gluten-free
for good

gluten-free
for good

simple, wholesome recipes
made from scratch

SAMANTHA SENEVIRATNE

Photographs by Stephen Kent Johnson

CLARKSON POTTER/PUBLISHERS
NEW YORK

Published in the United States by Clarkson Potter/Publishers, an
imprint of the Crown Publishing Group, a division of Penguin Random
House LLC, New York.
www.crownpublishing.com
www.clarksonpotter.com

CLARKSON POTTER is a trademark and POTTER with colophon is a
registered trademark of Penguin Random House LLC.

Library of Congress Cataloging-in-Publication Data is available upon
request.

ISBN 978-0-8041-8632-2
eBook ISBN 978-0-8041-8633-9

Printed in China

Cover and book design by La Tricia Watford
Cover photography by Stephen Kent Johnson

10 9 8 7 6 5 4 3 2 1

First Edition

contents

RECIPES

sweet and savory snacks 147

desserts   169

introduction

I love to feed people—family, friends, neighbors, colleagues, and just about anyone else who will eat my cooking—even more than I love to eat a good meal. There's no better feeling than satisfying hunger with food that brings others happiness. But these days, cooking for the people we care about seems to be getting trickier and trickier. Ten years ago, I had just one friend who was allergic to gluten. Now it seems like there are just as many people who avoid gluten as there are those who still eat it.

This may also be the case for you. And truth be told, cooking gluten-free can be hard to navigate. At first, it may seem as if everything you know about cooking must change and that your favorite foods have become the enemy overnight. A new diet can feel scary.

I know it can be tempting to rely on gluten-free packaged foods, a seemingly easy solution. Boxes of gluten-free cookies, crackers, pretzels, and cake mixes, and bags of gluten-free breads and pasta, now line the shelves everywhere. The freezer section is full of gluten-free desserts and ready-made piecrusts and pizzas. But convenience in this case can mean chemical preservatives, unnecessary gums, and extra sodium, sugar, and fat.

Unpronounceable additives are not the key to feeling good. And, more important, they are not the key to good flavor, either. And how could they be? Prepackaged store-bought gluten-free foods are impostors and forgeries of simple homemade foods.

I have a new plan for you. Get rid of the highly processed, high-priced fakes. Celebrate gluten-free ingredients for what they are: real foods with pleasures of their own. That means using them in ways that highlight the wonderful things they can bring to the table, not dressing them up as something they're not.

Making delicious homemade gluten-free food for breakfast, lunch, and dinner is easier than you might think. Remember that in every grocery store there are whole sections full of naturally gluten-free foods. Building dinners that start with vegetables, proteins, and gluten-free grains and seeds like rice, quinoa, and millet, for example, is an easy and nutritious way to go. As for the other foods that we all crave? Making gluten-free breads, pastas, and cookies is simple, too. In fact, cleaning out your freezer to create a little extra room for some alternative flours, all widely available, is probably the hardest part of the entire process.

I wrote this book with one goal in mind: to help you create tasty meals, mostly from scratch, that will please both gluten-free and conventional eaters alike. No meal should be defined by what's not there. Eating gluten-free should not mean having to say "It's pretty good—for being gluten-free." These wholesome, homemade, and delicious meals and snacks have value for everyone. So let's eat—together!

the gluten-free pantry

I used to cruise directly to the baking aisle of the supermarket to stock up on the one essential ingredient I always needed: all-purpose flour. The gluten-free section of the aisle was filled with shiny, exotic bags advertising interesting products I'd never heard of nor used, but I'd just skip by them. I would leave the store wondering if I'd ever know what sorghum flour tasted like or whether or not hazelnut flour was really as good as it sounded. Years later when I started experimenting with gluten-free cooking I realized what a fun opportunity I had! A whole section of the supermarket became an edible treasure trove and it was a thrill to start exploring.

There are so many exciting ingredients waiting for the fearless gluten-free cook. At first, abandoning the familiar may seem daunting. But I hope you'll be excited by the promise of delicious new flavors, textures, and aromas. Make some space in your cupboard and your freezer—it's going to be fun. Once your pantry is stocked and ready, you can think about storing a few simple building blocks in your fridge or freezer. See pages 20 through 31 for my Homemade Essentials, recipes that will add tons of flavor to your dishes.

STOCKING THE PANTRY

These days most well-stocked supermarkets and health food stores will carry just about any ingredient you may need to make wonderful gluten-free food. And if the supermarket fails you, you can probably find it on the Internet! We're lucky. I'm sure it wasn't so easy to cook gluten-free even a decade ago.

Here's a description of some of the ingredients that fill my pantry. The list may look long, but each ingredient plays a special role in gluten-free cooking. Not every ingredient is essential, but you'll find that a fully stocked pantry will give you more flexibility in creating delicious and wholesome gluten-free meals that satisfy everyone.

Please note that I am not a health professional. If you have a severe allergy to gluten, or specific needs and concerns, consult your doctor first. To be safe, look for *certified* gluten-free ingredients.

alternative flours

There are a number of gluten-free flour blends on the market, and believe me, I understand the time-saving appeal. But I don't use them in my recipes, and I'll tell you why.

First of all, different blends behave differently. Certain flour blends contain ingredients like gums that can be tricky for some people to digest (see page 19). Others include ingredients that have a strong flavor, which may be well suited for some recipes but not for others. And none of them seem to include healthful whole-grain gluten-free flours like sorghum and millet, which add nutritional value to plenty of baked goods. After hours and hours of testing gluten-free recipes, I've come to the conclusion that I can't rely on just one blend. And if that's the case, why even bother?

I also don't include a recipe for one all-purpose flour mix here. Instead, my recipes feature blends that suit the flavors of each dish. It all comes down to control. When you decide to make a meal from scratch, you give yourself the ability to customize your food exactly to your liking and your needs. To me—someone who really loves food—that makes the most sense.

---

tip If you have the space, store your gluten-free flours in the freezer and bring them back to room temperature before using. They will last much longer that way.

ALMOND FLOUR This is the queen of gluten-free baking—it's the most versatile gluten-free flour available. Made from ground blanched almonds, almond flour bakes beautifully in cakes and muffins—I use it in everything from pancakes to homemade crackers. Don't worry if almond's amaretto flavor isn't your thing; this flour tastes pleasantly neutral. My favorite brand is Honeyville for its lovely fine texture.

AMARANTH AND AMARANTH FLOUR A tiny seed native to South America, amaranth is chock-full of protein and vitamins, and so it makes a good addition to the gluten-free cupboard. Cook the whole grains for a nutritious breakfast porridge or pop them in a pot on the stovetop like popcorn for a fun snack. I use amaranth flour, made from ground seeds, to create a tender savory pastry crust.

CHICKPEA FLOUR Also called garbanzo bean flour, besan, or gram flour, chickpea flour is a good source of both protein and fiber. It is also one of the tastiest gluten-free flours around. I use it mostly for savory foods because I find the bean flavor too strong for sweets.

COCONUT FLOUR This high-fiber flour is made from dried defatted coconut meat. It has a very light coconut flavor and is great for baking. Coconut flour is very thirsty, so be sure to add extra liquid when using it (or just follow a recipe designed for coconut flour).

HAZELNUT FLOUR Also known as hazelnut meal, this flour is one of my absolute favorites. It's naturally delicious and makes extra-moist cakes and cookies. Preground hazelnut flour can be expensive, but thankfully it's easy to make at home. Simply toast the shelled hazelnuts on a baking sheet until the skins start to crack and separate from the nuts, about 10 minutes. Wrap the warm nuts in a clean dish towel and rub them vigorously. As they rub against each other, they'll peel themselves. Once the nuts have cooled completely, grind them to the consistency of flour in a food processor or spice grinder (don't go too far, or you'll end up with hazelnut butter).

MASA HARINA Masa harina is the flour made from hominy, the dried corn kernels that have been treated with a lime solution. Masa harina is used to make corn tortillas, tamales, and arepas, but it can also be added to soups and stews and used as a flavorful thickener.

MILK POWDER This is not exactly flour or a grain, but it is useful for gluten-free baking. Dried milk powder helps with the texture, shelf life, and color of gluten-free baked goods.

MILLET AND MILLET FLOUR You've most likely seen millet in bird feeders, but I urge you to think of it as more than just bird food. Also found in the grocery store, millet is a wonderfully versatile grain with a mild, sweet, corn-like flavor. I use the flour and whole uncooked grains in both sweet and savory baked goods. The whole grain also makes a nice side dish when cooked in an herb-laced broth. Millet has been a food staple in Africa and northern China for centuries. I think it's about time it gains popularity in the U.S., too!

OATS AND OAT FLOUR Oats are naturally gluten-free, which is why my recipes don't call for "gluten-free" oats or oat flour, but if you're particularly sensitive to gluten (or are cooking for someone who is), look for *certified* gluten-free oats and oat flour (conventional oats are often grown and processed near wheat, which can impart trace amounts of gluten). If you can't find gluten-free oat flour in the store, simply grind gluten-free oats to a fine powder in your blender, food processor, or spice grinder. Oats are a real win-win: they add a toasty, nutty flavor and are also proven to lower levels of "bad" cholesterol.

POTATO FLOUR Not to be confused with potato starch, potato flour is made from ground dried potatoes. It adds tenderness to baked goods and thickens soups and stews.

GROUND PSYLLIUM HUSK I love this stuff for adding structure and a little fiber to gluten-free breads. Psyllium husk is the outer coating of the seed of a plant called *Plantago ovata*. It is generally used as a fiber supplement, which is why it's often found in the health section of the supermarket. You can find it sold as either husks or a finely ground powder. The recipes in this book use the powder. I prefer Frontier brand; some brands can turn dough a funny shade of purple—which isn't harmful, just a little shocking.

QUINOA AND QUINOA FLOUR Known as "the mother of all grains" by the ancient Incans, this beloved seed has become a trendy super-food. Eating a big bowl of quinoa is a good way to get a healthy dose of protein, iron, magnesium, and fiber—not to mention that it's easy and fast to cook. It makes a delicious and nutritious weeknight replacement for pasta and couscous. Quinoa flour, made from the ground seeds, is a nutritious option, but I find the flavor of the flour too strong for baking.

RICE FLOUR Both brown and white rice flours have a place in the gluten-free pantry. Too much rice flour can lead to a gritty final product, but just the right amount adds structure and flavor. I've found that rice flours, both brown and white, can vary dramatically from brand to brand. For the best texture, I use Bob's Red Mill stone-ground rice flours exclusively. For the best value, buy them in bulk online and store them in the freezer.

SORGHUM AND SORGHUM FLOUR This drought-resistant grain, popular in Africa and Asia, is used in this country mostly as livestock feed and in the form of a syrup. But gluten-free eaters are catching on. The hearty grain has a pleasant nutty flavor and chewiness that's wonderful in salads. Full of protein, iron, and fiber, sorghum flour is excellent for gluten-free baking due to its smooth texture and mild flavor.

SWEET RICE FLOUR Also known as glutinous rice flour or mochiko, sweet rice flour is made by milling sticky rice to a fine powder. It is high in starch and does wonders for binding baked goods in the absence of gluten. I love it for making pasta from scratch. *Note:* Regular rice flour cannot be substituted for sweet rice flour.

starches

Chances are you've used starch before to thicken stews, pie fillings, and sauces. In gluten-free baking, they help add that elusive stretch that otherwise might be lost in the absence of wheat. These are a few of my favorites.

ARROWROOT STARCH This starch is extracted from *Maranta arundinacea*, a plant indigenous to the West Indies. Just like cornstarch, arrowroot starch is used as a thickener, but unlike cornstarch, it does not need a full boil to activate. In gluten-free baking, I use arrowroot starch and cornstarch interchangeably.

CORNSTARCH I bet you can guess where this starch comes from. Like other starches, it's useful in gluten-free cooking for adding tenderness; it also helps with binding. Cornstarch can be tricky if you're sensitive to gluten: like oats, cornstarch is sometimes processed in facilities that also process wheat. To be sure, look for *certified* gluten-free cornstarch.

POTATO STARCH While potato flour is made from the entire potato, potato starch is simply the isolated starch. In conventional cooking, it is usually used as a thickener. In gluten-free cooking, it adds tenderness to baked goods like breads and scones. Potato flour *cannot* be substituted for potato starch.

TAPIOCA FLOUR AND STARCH Just to make things really confusing, manufacturers label the same product as both tapioca flour and tapioca starch. Both are the starch of the cassava root, which is high in calcium and vitamin C. I like it for adding chew to gluten-free baked goods.

on gums

They may sound strange, but you've probably eaten xanthan gum and guar gum before. Gums are used in many supermarket items including toothpaste, canned coconut milk, ice cream, and salad dressing. They're often added to gluten-free recipes for their emulsifying and thickening properties. And they help to add structure in the absence of gluten. Some people find gums difficult to digest. For that reason, none of the recipes in this book include any gums.

Xanthan gum

When the bacteria *Xanthomonas campestris* is allowed to ferment with corn sugar, it creates a gel. That gel is dried and milled to make xanthan gum, which is commonly used as an emulsifier and a thickener in processed foods. It's also helpful for adding structure to gluten-free baked goods, especially those requiring yeast.

Guar gum

Guar gum is another binder popular in gluten-free baking. It's derived from the ground endosperm of the guar bean.

Surprisingly, some canned chicken broths are not gluten-free. Making chicken broth from scratch is easy and safer for anyone who is gluten-intolerant. It's also considerably more delicious.

chicken broth

MAKES ABOUT 8 CUPS

2½ pounds chicken bones

3 medium carrots, scrubbed and cut into 2-inch pieces

1 medium onion, cut into 1-inch wedges

4 stalks celery, cut into 2-inch pieces

1 small bunch parsley stems

3 fresh bay leaves (or 6 dried leaves)

1 teaspoon peppercorns

1 Combine all the ingredients in a large stockpot and add 16 cups (4 quarts) of water. Bring to a boil, then reduce to a very low simmer and cook for 3 to 4 hours, occasionally skimming off the gray foam. You are looking for golden yellow color and a rich chicken flavor. (I like to taste a spoonful with a little seasoning to decide when my broth is ready.) If the liquid seems to be reducing too quickly, cover the pot partially with a lid.

2 Let the broth cool to room temperature; then strain it and pour it into quart-sized containers. Keep it in the fridge for up to 1 week or in the freezer for up to 2 months.

This full-flavored vegetable broth is well suited for robust dishes like hearty vegetable stews and earthy mushroom risottos. For a milder vegetable broth, just skip the roasting step.

roasted vegetable broth

MAKES ABOUT 8 CUPS

6 medium carrots, scrubbed and cut into 2-inch pieces

8 small stalks celery, cut into 2-inch pieces

2 medium onions, cut into 1-inch wedges

1 pound button mushrooms, halved

¼ cup neutral oil, such as safflower

1 small bunch parsley stems

1 teaspoon peppercorns

3 fresh bay leaves (or 6 dried leaves)

2 to 3 tablespoons gluten-free tamari

1 Preheat the oven to 400°F. Spread the carrots, celery, onions, and mushrooms onto two large rimmed baking sheets. Drizzle with the oil and toss to coat. Roast until the vegetables have browned, turning occasionally, 50 to 60 minutes. You want golden brown vegetables without any char.

2 Transfer the vegetables to a large stockpot. Pour 1 cup of water onto each of the baking sheets and use a wooden spoon to scrape up all the browned bits. Pour that liquid into the stockpot. Add the parsley, peppercorns, bay leaves, and an additional 14 cups (3½ quarts) of water. Bring the mixture to a boil, reduce the heat to a gentle simmer, and cook the broth for 1 to 2 hours. You are looking for deep golden brown color and a good vegetable flavor. (I like to taste a spoonful with a little seasoning to decide when my broth is ready.) If the liquid seems to be reducing too quickly, cover the pot partially with a lid.

3 Let the broth cool to room temperature; then strain out the vegetables and seasonings, and stir in the tamari to taste. (The broth doesn't need to taste salty, just rich.) Pour the broth into quart-sized containers. Keep it in the fridge for up to 1 week or in the freezer for up to 2 months.

Za'atar is a Middle Eastern and Mediterranean spice blend that usually includes sesame seeds, sumac, and dried herbs. I like to make it using fresh herbs—the flavor is so much brighter. Za'atar is very versatile stuff: sprinkle it over a roast chicken, potatoes (see page 75), and other vegetables, or even just a simple plate of scrambled eggs (see page 54). I even use it to flavor homemade potato chips.

fresh herb za'atar

MAKES A SCANT ¼ CUP

1 tablespoon chopped fresh thyme leaves

1 tablespoon chopped fresh oregano leaves

1 tablespoon sesame seeds, toasted (see Tip, page 31)

2 teaspoons ground sumac (see Cooking with Sumac)

½ teaspoon kosher salt

1 In a mortar, combine the thyme, oregano, sesame seeds, sumac, and salt. Use the pestle to pound the mixture together until the herbs are bruised and some of the sesame seeds are broken down. (A few pulses in a spice grinder will also do the trick.)

2 Za'atar will keep in an airtight container at room temperature for up to 2 weeks.

cooking with sumac

Long ago, before the Romans brought lemons to Europe, people used sumac to add tartness to their foods. Native to the Middle East, sumac bushes produce bright red berries that are dried and ground into powder. Look for it in the spice section of a well-stocked or specialty supermarket. If you're lucky enough to find fresh berries, steep them lightly in hot water to make a tangy sumac tea.

Harissa is a pepper paste that is traditionally used in North African and Middle Eastern dishes. I stir it into hearty salads like French Lentil and Harissa Salad (page 88), into hummus, and into soups and stews. It also makes a nice condiment alongside roasted meats and is a tasty sandwich spread. It can range from sweet and mild to face-meltingly spicy. I like mine somewhere in the middle, so this recipe is fairly mild, with roasted red bell pepper, medium-hot pasilla chiles, and smoky anchos (dried poblanos), but you can use whatever dried chiles you like. For a little more heat, swap in some New Mexico chiles, chipotles, or even a few fresh Thai bird chiles.

mild harissa

½ ounce chile negro (pasilla) chiles (about 4), stemmed and seeded (see Tip)

½ ounce ancho chiles (about 2), stemmed and seeded (see Tip)

1 medium red bell pepper

1 teaspoon caraway seeds

1 teaspoon cumin seeds

2 teaspoons coriander seeds

4 garlic cloves

2 teaspoons kosher salt

1 teaspoon finely grated lemon zest

2 tablespoons fresh lemon juice

2 tablespoons extra virgin olive oil, plus extra for coating the top

---

tip It's best to wear gloves when working with hot chiles as their oily residue can stick to your fingers long after you've finished the task.

1 Bring a small pot of water to a boil. Combine the dried chiles in a heatproof bowl and cover with the boiling water. Cover the bowl with plastic wrap and set it aside for the chiles to soften, 1 hour.

2 Meanwhile, roast the red bell pepper by setting it directly over the gas flame of your stove, rotating it often with tongs, until softened and charred all over, about 25 minutes. (Alternatively, set the pepper on a foil-lined baking sheet about 4 inches from the broiler set on high, turning every 3 to 5 minutes until softened and charred, 15 to 20 minutes.) Transfer the pepper to a bowl, cover it with plastic wrap, and set it aside until the pepper is cool enough to handle, about 15 minutes.

3 Put the caraway, cumin, and coriander seeds in a dry skillet, and heat over medium heat until toasted and fragrant, about 3 minutes. Then grind them in a spice grinder.

4 Peel the blackened skin off the red bell pepper and discard it. Remove and discard the stem and the seeds. Transfer the pepper to the bowl of a food processor. Drain the soaked chiles and add them to the processor. Add the ground spices along with the garlic, salt, lemon zest, lemon juice, and olive oil. Process until smooth. Transfer the harissa to a jar and pour a thin layer of olive oil over the top. Keep the harissa in the fridge for up to 1 month.

fresh herb
za'atar

mild harissa

preserved
meyer lemons

Fresh lemons are the workhorses of my kitchen and I use them in practically everything. Sweet, thin-skinned Meyer lemons are even more special. You can find them in most grocery stores. Making them takes a bit of foresight, but a long soak in salt and spices makes them irresistible: the lemons break down and become silky as their flavor intensifies. Some people rinse off the salt before using the lemons, but I add them as is. Just be sure to adjust the seasoning in the recipe.

MAKES 1 PINT

3 Meyer lemons, plus 1 to 2 more if necessary, scrubbed

Kosher salt or sea salt

1 teaspoon coriander seeds (optional)

1 bay leaf (optional)

preserved meyer lemons

1 Slice one eighth of the stem end off 1 lemon. Starting from the cut end, slice the lemon in half, stopping about ¼ inch from the bottom. Cut another slice perpendicular to the first cut. Repeat with the other 2 lemons.

2 Unfold each lemon and sprinkle salt generously on all of the cut sides. Sprinkle some salt into the bottom of a 1-pint jar and add the coriander seeds, if using. Add 1 lemon to the jar, cut (stem) end down, and press it well, squeezing out some of the juice. Tuck the bay leaf, if using, next to the lemon. Add the remaining 2 lemons in the same way.

3 The juice should reach to about ⅛ inch below the top of the jar and should submerge all of the fruit. If it doesn't, add the juice of 1 or 2 more lemons. Refrigerate the covered jar for at least 1 month, shaking it occasionally throughout the first week.

tip The preserved lemons need to rest in the fridge for at least a month, but the longer you keep them after that, the better the flavor.

Labneh is a creamy strained yogurt cheese known in one form or another in many Middle Eastern countries. It tastes like a tangy cross between cream cheese and yogurt. It's simply wonderful and easy to make at home by straining plain yogurt. The longer you strain it, the thicker it will get. I like it best after about 14 hours, when it's thick and luscious but still creamy. Serve it sprinkled with za'atar (see page 22) and olive oil as a simple dip. You can also stir it into eggs (see page 54) or use it to make a creamy salad dressing (see page 94). It makes a decadent dessert when topped with bananas and honey, or a delicious summer pasta with orzo and fresh herbs. Strain it even longer and the cheese will be so thick that you can roll it into balls. Marinate them in olive oil, herbs, and garlic for a lovely appetizer.

MAKES ABOUT ½ CUP

2 cups whole-milk plain yogurt

¾ teaspoon kosher salt

labneh

1 Set a medium sieve over a bowl, and line the sieve with several layers of cheesecloth. Add the yogurt to the sieve and stir in the salt.

2 Fold the cheesecloth up and over the yogurt, making sure the yogurt is well covered. Set a small bowl on top of the covered yogurt to weight it down.

3 Refrigerate for at least 8 hours for a creamy cheese and up to about 48 hours for labneh balls. Keep it in an airtight container in the fridge for up to 1 week.

We all owe Julia Child a debt of gratitude for teaching Americans to make mayonnaise in the 1960s. Buying a jar at the supermarket may be easy, but what you save in convenience you lose in flavor—not to mention satisfaction! Whipping up fresh mayonnaise takes only a bit of extra effort, and it tastes so good. It makes you feel like a magician in your own kitchen. Stir in some mashed garlic, fresh herbs, saffron, or capers to make your mayonnaise extra-fancy.

lemony mayonnaise

MAKES ABOUT ⅔ CUP

1 large egg yolk

1½ teaspoons gluten-free Dijon mustard

½ cup neutral oil, such as safflower or vegetable oil

2 teaspoons fresh lemon juice

Kosher salt

1 In a medium bowl, whisk together the egg yolk and the mustard. While whisking, slowly add the oil, a drop at a time to start and then in a very thin stream, stopping occasionally to make sure the oil is incorporated. Add the lemon juice and salt to taste.

2 Keep the mayonnaise in an airtight container in the fridge for up to 1 week.

It's a wonder that two simple ingredients—salt and sesame seeds—and a little elbow grease can create a condiment that is so incredibly tasty and versatile. It's nice sprinkled on practically anything: roasted vegetables, salads, even popcorn.

gomasio

MAKES ABOUT ¼ CUP

4 tablespoons sesame seeds, toasted (see Tip, page 31)

½ teaspoon kosher salt

1 Combine the sesame seeds and the salt in a mortar. Use the pestle to grind the mixture together until about two thirds of the seeds are broken down. (Alternatively, use a spice grinder.)

2 Store in an airtight container at room temperature or in the fridge for up to 2 weeks.

Homemade ricotta has so much more flavor than the stuff you buy at the store. If you use ultra-pasteurized milk and cream, the ricotta will be thick and smooth. Use less pasteurized milk and cream for a more textured result. (Both are tasty, so don't worry too much about it.) Stir this ricotta into pasta sauce, or top it with fruit and eat it for breakfast. I love it with jam on toast—one of life's simplest and most delicious pleasures.

fresh ricotta

MAKES 1½ CUPS

2½ cups whole milk

1½ cups heavy cream

1½ teaspoons kosher salt

3 tablespoons fresh lemon juice, plus more if necessary

1 Set a medium sieve over a bowl, and line the sieve with a couple of layers of cheesecloth.

2 Bring the milk, cream, and salt to a simmer in a saucepan over medium-high heat, stirring occasionally. Don't walk away! You don't want it to boil over.

3 Add the lemon juice to the hot milk mixture, and stir until the mixture curdles, 1 to 2 minutes. Pour the mixture into the sieve and set it aside to drain, stirring occasionally to help it along, 30 minutes to 1 hour. The longer the ricotta strains, the thicker it will be. Store the strained ricotta in a covered container in the fridge for up to 1 week. It will thicken up further as it cools.

tip If the mixture refuses to curdle after you add the lemon juice, try adding a little bit more juice, about a teaspoon at a time.

I use canned beans all the time. But when I have time, I like to cook a pot of dried beans. The beans taste earthy and extra-beany (for lack of a better word) when cooked from dry. Not to mention that I don't have to clean off that mysterious salty sludge that coats canned beans.

pot of beans

MAKES 5 CUPS

1 pound dried beans

Kosher salt

2 bay leaves

3 garlic cloves, smashed

½ yellow onion, cut into thick wedges

1 Put the beans in a large pot and add enough cold water to cover them by 2 inches. Stir in a generous pinch of salt. Set aside to soak at room temperature for at least 12 hours and up to 24.

2 Preheat the oven to 300°F. Drain the beans. Place them in a large oven-safe pot and add the bay leaves, garlic, and onions. Add enough fresh water to cover the ingredients by 2 inches, and stir in 1 teaspoon salt.

3 Bring the water to a boil; then cover the pot and transfer it to the oven. Cook for between 45 minutes and 2 hours, depending on the size of the beans. Smaller beans, such as cannellini beans, usually need less cooking time, so start checking them for doneness after 30 minutes. Let the beans cool in their cooking liquid, then transfer the beans and the liquid to an airtight container. Store them in the fridge for 1 week or in the freezer for up to 3 months.

tips

• If you forget to soak your beans the night before, try the quick-soak method: Bring the beans and plenty of water to a boil in a saucepan. Remove the pan from the heat and let it stand, covered, for 1 hour. Then drain the beans and proceed with the recipe.

• Instead of pouring the leftover cooking liquid down the drain, use it as a base for a soup or a flavorful pot of rice and beans.

I love tahini, the nutty sesame paste, as much as the next girl. But why is it sold in such huge tubs? They're impossible to finish and take up too much valuable real estate in the fridge. It was only while cursing a giant tin of the stuff that I realized how simple it would be to make it from scratch. Sesame seeds are relatively inexpensive and just need a quick toasting to become tahini-ready. This recipe makes a modest ½ cup, enough for a few uses, but if you want more, it doubles easily.

tahini

MAKES ABOUT ½ CUP

1 cup sesame seeds, toasted (see Tip)

1 teaspoon kosher salt

¼ cup neutral oil, such as safflower

1 Place the sesame seeds and the salt in the bowl of a food processor fitted with the metal blade. With the processor running, pour the oil in through the feed tube. Process the mixture until smooth.

2 Store the tahini in an airtight container in the fridge for up to 1 month. The oil may separate, but that's normal. Just stir it back together.

---

tip Toast sesame seeds in a dry skillet over medium heat, stirring often, until golden brown, 3 to 5 minutes.

breakfast and brunch

"Can you make us a *wholesome* breakfast?" That was the request my brother and I would ask of our mom on lazy Saturday mornings when we were kids. We'd all still be in our pajamas—my poor mom just trying to enjoy her cup of tea—when we'd start to beg. The weekdays were for cereal. The weekend was for something warm, creamy, and cozy. We wanted a breakfast that would fill us up and make us feel sated and cared for. Sometimes she'd scramble eggs with tomatoes, curry leaves, and chiles. Other times she made oatmeal with brown sugar and berries, or Cream of Wheat with salty butter and bananas. We didn't care if it was fancy. To us, wholesome just meant made with love: a hug in breakfast form.

Nowadays when I make breakfast, I still think about the word "wholesome." A nutritious breakfast, made with love and care, is a generous gift to those you cook for—especially those with a gluten intolerance or sensitivity. In this chapter I've given you plenty of gluten-free options to satisfy all kinds of eaters. If you have company, try the tender Cinnamon Buns (page 43) or the Blueberry Streusel Cake (page 40). For something equally delicious but savory, turn to the Roasted Tomatoes with Labneh, Soft Scrambled Eggs, and Za'atar (page 54) or Smoked Gouda Grits (page 56). Or maybe you like to plan ahead: warm Raspberry Hazelnut Scones (page 51) are oven-ready when you've frozen them in advance. All these breakfasts start good days, guaranteed.

The tartness of the apples and the deep, roasted sweetness of the molasses in these muffins bring to mind the coziness of fall and winter. Crisp pears would also be nice.

apple molasses muffins

MAKES 12 MUFFINS

1¾ cups (160 g) almond flour

¾ cup (80 g) oat flour

2 teaspoons baking powder

¼ teaspoon baking soda

¾ teaspoon kosher salt

2 large eggs, separated

⅓ cup molasses

¼ cup plain whole-milk yogurt

2 tablespoons light brown sugar

2 teaspoons pure vanilla extract

2 teaspoons finely grated orange zest (from 1 orange)

1 medium apple, such as McIntosh, Honeycrisp, or Granny Smith, cored and diced (1½ cups)

1 Preheat the oven to 400°F. Line a standard 12-cup muffin pan with paper liners. In a medium bowl, whisk together the almond flour, oat flour, baking powder, baking soda, and salt.

2 In a large bowl, whisk together the egg yolks, molasses, yogurt, brown sugar, vanilla, and orange zest. Stir the flour mixture into the egg mixture. Fold in the apple.

3 In a medium bowl, with a clean whisk or with an electric mixer on medium speed, beat the egg whites until stiff peaks form, about 2 minutes. Stir a third of the egg whites into the batter to loosen it; then carefully fold the remaining egg whites into the batter.

4 Divide the batter evenly among the muffin cups. Transfer the pan to the oven and immediately reduce the temperature to 350°F. Bake until the muffins spring back when pressed gently, 18 to 20 minutes. Let the muffins cool in the pan for 5 minutes, and then transfer them to a rack to cool completely.

Going gluten-free doesn't mean you have to give up bread. And it's easier than you think to make it from scratch. I'm as thrilled as you are! This hearty, honey-kissed sandwich bread tastes great right out of the oven. It's even nice eaten fresh for the first and second days—no need to toast it until the third day. A single slice of bread topped with butter, cheese, fruit, or vegetables can be a real masterpiece for breakfast, but it's also my favorite treat for an elegant solo dinner.

a simple loaf of bread

MAKES 1 LOAF

1 cup whole milk

3 tablespoons honey

5 tablespoons unsalted butter, cut into pieces, plus more for the pan

¾ cup (80 g) oat flour

¾ cup (105 g) white rice flour

¾ cup (135 g) potato starch

½ cup (70 g) millet flour

½ cup (60 g) tapioca starch

3 tablespoons psyllium husk powder

2 teaspoons baking powder

1¾ teaspoons instant yeast

1½ teaspoons kosher salt

3 large eggs, at room temperature

1 large egg white

1 Bring the milk just to a boil in a small pot over medium heat, watching closely to ensure that it doesn't boil over. Transfer the hot milk to a small bowl and add the honey and the butter; stir to completely dissolve. Let the mixture cool to 105° to 110°F. (It should be warm to the touch but not too hot.)

2 Butter an 8½ × 4½-inch loaf pan.

3 In the bowl of a stand mixer, whisk together the oat flour, white rice flour, potato starch, millet flour, tapioca starch, psyllium husk powder, baking powder, yeast, and salt. Using the paddle attachment with the mixer on low speed, add the milk mixture to the flour mixture. Mix until the flour mixture is evenly moistened. Mix in the eggs, one at a time, scraping down the bowl as needed. Increase the speed to medium and beat until the dough is well combined, 3 to 4 minutes.

4 Scrape down the sides of the bowl and transfer the dough to the prepared loaf pan. With wet fingers, spread it out. Use a wet plastic dough scraper or offset spatula to smooth the top of the dough. Cover the pan with plastic wrap and let the dough rise to about ¾ inch above the rim of the pan, about 1 hour. (This could take a little bit longer if your house is chilly.) After about 40 minutes of rising, preheat the oven to 350°F.

(RECIPE CONTINUES)

5 In a small bowl, mix the egg white with 1 tablespoon of water. Very gently brush the top of the loaf with this egg wash. Bake the loaf until it is deep golden brown and set, 1 hour 15 minutes to 1 hour 30 minutes, covering the top of the loaf with foil if it browns too quickly. Set the pan on a rack to cool for a few minutes, and then tip the loaf out. Cool the loaf completely on the rack before slicing.

fresh ricotta, page 28

Here almonds and oats come together to make a quick batter that's both light and flavorful. I love wild blueberries in my pancakes, but you can substitute whatever seasonal fruit you have on hand. If you have leftovers, pop them into the freezer. A frozen pancake toasts up into a treat on hurried mornings.

almond oat pancakes with blueberries and lemon

**SERVES 4
(MAKES ABOUT 12 PANCAKES)**

1½ cups (135 g) almond flour

¾ cup (80 g) oat flour

2¼ teaspoons baking powder

½ teaspoon kosher salt

¾ cup whole milk

2 large eggs, lightly beaten

4 teaspoons honey

2½ teaspoons finely grated lemon zest

1½ cups fresh blueberries, preferably wild

Butter or coconut oil, for the skillet

Maple syrup, for serving

1 Preheat the oven to 200°F. In a medium bowl, whisk together the almond flour, oat flour, baking powder, and salt. While whisking, add the milk in a slow stream. Then add the eggs, honey, and lemon zest, and stir to combine. Fold in the blueberries.

2 Melt a pat of butter in a large nonstick skillet over medium-high heat. Working in batches, drop ¼ cup of the batter into the skillet to form each pancake. Cook until the edges of the underside are golden brown, 2 to 3 minutes. Flip the pancakes and cook until the underside is golden brown, adjusting the heat as needed, 2 to 3 minutes more.

3 Transfer the pancakes to a baking sheet and keep them warm in the oven. Repeat with more butter and the remaining batter, wiping the skillet clean with a paper towel between batches. Serve with maple syrup.

Nothing goes better with a cup of coffee than a big slab of streusel cake. Here I use a combination of almond flour and oat flour, which adds both flavor and fiber. I keep frozen wild blueberries on hand at all times. They are far more delicious for baking than conventional berries. You don't even have to thaw them before using them: just throw them into the batter frozen. If you're lucky enough to find fresh wild blueberries, reduce the baking time by a few minutes.

blueberry streusel cake

SERVES 10 TO 12

TOPPING

2 tablespoons unsalted butter, at room temperature, plus more for the pan

¼ cup packed dark brown sugar

½ cup old-fashioned rolled oats

¼ teaspoon kosher salt

½ cup pecans, toasted and chopped

BATTER

2½ cups (225 g) almond flour

½ cup (50 g) oat flour

¼ cup arrowroot starch

2 teaspoons baking powder

1 teaspoon kosher salt

½ teaspoon ground cardamom or cinnamon

¼ cup packed dark brown sugar

¼ cup maple syrup

½ cup plain whole-milk yogurt

4 large eggs, separated

1 teaspoon finely grated lemon zest (from 1 lemon)

2 cups fresh or frozen blueberries, preferably wild (see Tip)

tip Frozen or fresh cranberries make a nice substitute in the fall.

1 Preheat the oven to 350°F. Butter a 9-inch springform pan with a removable bottom.

2 **Make the topping:** In a small bowl, combine the brown sugar, oats, and salt. Beat in the butter. Stir in the nuts.

3 **Prepare the batter:** In a large bowl, whisk together the almond flour, oat flour, arrowroot starch, baking powder, salt, and cardamom. Add the brown sugar, maple syrup, yogurt, and egg yolks, and stir to combine.

4 In a large clean bowl, with an electric mixer, beat the egg whites on medium speed until stiff peaks form. Stir a quarter of the whites into the almond mixture to loosen the batter, and then fold in the remaining whites. Fold in the lemon zest and blueberries. Transfer the batter to the prepared pan. Sprinkle the streusel over the top of the cake, using your fingers to squeeze the streusel into clumps as you go.

5 Bake until the cake is golden brown and a toothpick inserted into the center comes out with moist crumbs attached, 50 to 60 minutes. Cover the pan with foil if the topping starts to get too dark before the center is set. Transfer the pan to a rack to cool for about 15 minutes; then remove the pan sides and let the cake cool completely.

Brown rice adds wonderful texture, heft, and a bit of fiber to this brunch favorite—not to mention that it's a great way to use up leftovers! I opt for Canadian bacon over regular bacon for a lean version that packs a lot of flavor. You could also use some thinly sliced ham. If you have them on hand, baby arugula or spinach leaves dressed with lemon and oil make a pretty and delicious topping.

brown rice frittata with canadian bacon and fontina

SERVES 4 TO 6

3 teaspoons olive oil

4 slices gluten-free uncured Canadian bacon

1 small yellow onion, cut into small dice

8 large eggs

¼ cup whole milk

6 tablespoons grated Fontina cheese

2 tablespoons chopped fresh basil leaves

Kosher salt and freshly ground black pepper

1 cup frozen peas, thawed

1 cup cooked brown rice

1 Preheat the oven to 300°F. In a 10-inch oven-safe skillet, heat 1½ teaspoons of the oil over medium-high heat. Add the bacon and cook until browned on both sides, about 2 minutes per side. Transfer the bacon to a cutting board and dice it.

2 In the same skillet over medium heat, add the remaining 1½ teaspoons oil and the onions and cook, stirring, until the onions are soft, about 5 minutes.

3 Meanwhile, in a large bowl, whisk together the eggs, milk, 4 tablespoons of the Fontina, 1 tablespoon of the basil, and the bacon. Season with salt and pepper to taste.

4 Add the peas and rice to the onions, and cook until the rice is warmed through, 2 to 3 minutes. Add the egg mixture and swirl it around to distribute everything evenly and start the cooking process. Sprinkle with the remaining 2 tablespoons of Fontina. Cook until the frittata is just set on the bottom, 1 minute. Then transfer the skillet to the oven and cook until the frittata is completely set, 24 to 26 minutes. Sprinkle with the remaining basil before serving.

One dreary New York February, I got so carried away making cinnamon buns that my gas bill practically tripled. The oven was always on! No kidding—I couldn't stop creating variations with fruit and chocolate, experimenting with different rising techniques, and creating new doughs every week. Rolling and slicing puffy dough became an addiction. I guess there are worse things.

This gluten-free version took quite a few tests to perfect, but I finally came up with a lovely bun worth making over and over again. I hope this combination of tender dough, fragrant filling, and a creamy, sweet glaze becomes a new obsession for you, too.

cinnamon buns

DOUGH

1 cup whole milk

⅓ cup neutral oil, such as safflower

1 large egg

1 tablespoon pure vanilla extract

1 cup (140 g) white rice flour

1 cup (120 g) sorghum flour

1 cup (180 g) potato starch

¾ cup (90 g) tapioca starch, plus more for the work surface

½ cup (60 g) milk powder

½ cup granulated sugar

¼ cup psyllium husk powder

2¼ teaspoons instant yeast

1 teaspoon kosher salt

Butter, for the baking dish

1 Make the dough: Bring the milk just to a boil in a small pot over medium heat, watching closely to ensure that it doesn't boil over. Transfer the hot milk to a 2-cup liquid measuring cup and add 1 or 2 tablespoons of warm water, enough to measure exactly 1 cup. Then add ⅔ cup warm water and let the mixture cool to 105° to 110°F. (It should be warm to the touch but not too hot.) Add the oil, egg, and vanilla; stir to combine.

2 In the bowl of a stand mixer, whisk together the rice flour, sorghum flour, potato starch, tapioca starch, milk powder, sugar, psyllium husk powder, yeast, and salt until well combined.

3 With the paddle attachment on low speed, add the milk mixture to the flour mixture and continue to beat until the mixture is smooth. Increase the speed to medium and beat for another 4 minutes. The dough will be wet and sticky and look like cookie dough. Scrape down the sides of the bowl and cover it with plastic wrap. Let the dough rest for 5 minutes.

4 Lightly butter a 9 × 13-inch baking pan and set it aside.

(RECIPE CONTINUES)

FILLING

½ cup packed dark brown sugar

3 tablespoons ground cinnamon

½ teaspoon kosher salt

4 tablespoons (½ stick) unsalted
butter, at room temperature

EGG WASH

1 large egg

1 tablespoon heavy cream
(optional)

GLAZE

6 ounces cream cheese,
at room temperature

3 tablespoons unsalted butter, at
room temperature

⅓ cup confectioners' sugar

2 to 3 tablespoons whole milk

½ teaspoon pure vanilla extract

5 Prepare the filling: Combine the brown sugar, cinnamon, and salt in a small bowl, and set it aside.

6 Lightly cover a work surface with tapioca starch. Scrape the dough onto the prepared surface and pat it out to a ½-inch-thick rectangle that measures 12 × 10 inches. Spread the butter evenly over the surface of the dough, sprinkle it with the brown sugar mixture, and pat it gently to adhere. Starting with one of the long sides, roll the dough up and over itself into a tight log, brushing off any excess tapioca flour as you roll it.

7 Use a serrated knife to slice the log into 12 equal pieces. (Use a light touch to quickly saw through the log instead of pushing down on the knife.) Carefully transfer the pieces to the prepared baking pan, cut side down. Cover with plastic wrap and set in a warm spot to rise until the buns look puffier and touch one another, about 1 hour. Preheat the oven to 375°F.

8 Make the egg wash: In a small bowl, whisk the egg with the cream, if using, or with 1 tablespoon of water. Gently brush the egg wash over the buns. Bake the buns until they are golden brown and set, 20 to 22 minutes.

9 Meanwhile, prepare the glaze: Beat together the cream cheese, butter, and confectioners' sugar in a small bowl. Add the milk and vanilla, and beat until smooth.

10 Let the buns cool slightly, then top them with the glaze before serving. These are best served warm the day they're made. If you have leftovers, warm them wrapped in foil in a low oven or for 20 to 30 seconds in the microwave.

I love Dutch babies, the big skillet pancake with crispy, buttery edges and a warm custardy center. My version uses fresh pears and real vanilla to create a sweet, fragrant breakfast treat. A perfect Dutch baby will puff around the edges while baking.

dutch baby with vanilla and pear

SERVES 2 TO 4

¼ cup brown rice flour

¼ cup almond flour

3 tablespoons tapioca starch

¼ teaspoon kosher salt

3 large eggs, at room temperature

¾ cup whole milk, at room temperature

½ teaspoon pure vanilla extract

2 tablespoons unsalted butter

2 tablespoons granulated sugar

1 large Bosc pear, peeled, cored, and cut into ¼-inch-thick slices

1 vanilla bean, split, seeds scraped out and reserved

Confectioners' sugar, for serving

1 Place a 10-inch cast-iron skillet on a rack about 6 inches below the oven broiler. Preheat the oven to 450°F. Meanwhile, in a large bowl, whisk together the brown rice flour, almond flour, tapioca starch, and salt. In a small bowl, whisk together the eggs, milk, and vanilla. Slowly add the milk mixture to the flour mixture while whisking until smooth. Set the batter aside.

2 After about 20 minutes, when the skillet and the oven are hot, carefully remove the skillet and switch the oven to broil. Add the butter to the hot skillet and swirl it around. Sprinkle the granulated sugar evenly over the butter. Add the pear slices and vanilla bean seeds, and toss to coat.

3 Return the skillet to the oven and broil until the sugar begins to caramelize, stirring halfway through, 4 to 5 minutes. Remove the skillet from the oven and turn the oven temperature back to 450°F.

4 Whisk the batter and immediately add it to the skillet. Return the skillet to the oven and cook until the Dutch baby is puffed and set, 12 to 16 minutes. Sprinkle it with confectioners' sugar before serving.

---

tip Make sure that all your ingredients are at room temperature and your skillet is nice and hot. The Dutch baby will deflate as it cools but will continue to taste wonderful.

It took me forever to decide on the best time for serving this treat. Is it dessert or is it breakfast? Is it a cake or is it bread? Such tough choices! I settled on putting it out for breakfast. It looks indulgent and tastes sweet, but it's also full of healthful ingredients that make for a good start to the day. Instead of the glaze, you could top a slice with some plain yogurt, granola, and fresh fruit—a breakfast sundae!

maple-glazed butternut squash bread

SERVES 16

BATTER

1 small butternut squash (1 to 2 pounds), halved and seeds scraped out

¼ cup melted coconut oil, plus more for the pan (see Tip, page 175)

1½ cups (135 g) almond flour

1½ cups (155 g) oat flour

2 teaspoons ground cinnamon

1½ teaspoons baking powder

1 teaspoon kosher salt

½ teaspoon baking soda

⅓ cup packed dark brown sugar

⅓ cup maple syrup

4 large eggs, separated

GLAZE (OPTIONAL)

1 cup confectioners' sugar

6 tablespoons maple syrup

2 tablespoons melted coconut oil

Pinch of kosher salt

½ cup toasted pecans or walnuts, chopped

1 Preheat the oven to 400°F. Set the squash halves, cut side down, on a parchment-lined baking sheet. Roast until the flesh is tender, 50 to 60 minutes, flipping over the halves halfway through. When the squash is cool enough to handle, scoop the flesh into the bowl of a food processor and process until smooth. Measure ¾ cup squash puree for the recipe (reserve the rest for another recipe or add some butter and salt and eat it for lunch). Reduce the oven temperature to 350°F. Oil a 9-inch square cake pan and line it with parchment, leaving a 2-inch overhang on two sides.

2 **Prepare the batter:** Whisk together the almond flour, oat flour, cinnamon, baking powder, salt, and baking soda in a medium bowl. In a large bowl, stir together the brown sugar and the coconut oil. Stir in the squash puree and the maple syrup. Add the egg yolks and whisk to combine. Fold the dry ingredients into the wet ingredients, and set aside.

(RECIPE CONTINUES)

3 In a clean bowl, using an electric mixer fitted with clean beaters, beat the egg whites to medium peaks (they should be stiff but not dry), 2 to 3 minutes. Stir a third of the egg whites into the batter to loosen it; then carefully fold the remaining egg whites into the batter. Transfer the batter to the prepared cake pan. Bake until a toothpick inserted into the center comes out with moist crumbs attached, 45 to 55 minutes. Transfer the pan to a rack to cool.

4 Meanwhile, prepare the glaze, if desired: Whisk together the confectioners' sugar, maple syrup, coconut oil, salt, and enough water (just a drop or two) to make a smooth, pourable glaze. Using the parchment, lift the cake out of the pan. Drizzle the glaze over the top; then sprinkle it with the nuts. Let it stand at room temperature to set before serving.

Traditionally muesli is an unsweetened mix of oats, nuts, and dried fruit. It's granola's lighter, simpler cousin. I like to toast mine and add plenty of warm spices for a deeper flavor. There are as many ways to eat muesli as there are to make it. My favorite is to give it an overnight soak in plain yogurt and then top it with fruit before serving. Or skip the soak and enjoy it fresh with cold or warm milk and a drizzle of maple syrup. For a dairy-free version, you can soak it in some freshly squeezed fruit juice or almond milk.

toasted muesli with dates and walnuts

MAKES 3 CUPS

2 cups old-fashioned rolled oats

⅔ cup walnut halves

½ teaspoon freshly ground cardamom

½ teaspoon ground cinnamon

2 tablespoons flaxseed meal

½ teaspoon kosher salt

4 ounces dried Medjool dates (about 8), pitted and chopped (see Tip, page 196)

1 Preheat the oven to 350°F. Spread the oats out over two thirds of a rimmed baking sheet. On the remaining third, spread out the walnuts. Bake until the walnuts are fragrant, about 8 minutes. Transfer the walnuts to a cutting board and continue to toast the oats until they just start to take on a little bit more color, another 10 to 12 minutes.

2 In a large bowl, toss the warm oats with the cardamom and cinnamon. Let the oats cool completely. Finely chop the walnuts.

3 Toss the oats with the flaxseed meal, salt, dates, and walnuts. (Sometimes it helps to use your hands if the dates clump together.) Transfer the mixture to an airtight container that you can shake to redistribute the goodies in the muesli before serving. Store at room temperature for up to 1 month.

My idea of heaven includes a cup of tea, a good book, and something to nibble on. These scones often play a part in this luxurious fantasy. The sweet, rich hazelnut flour is a lovely addition to the craggy biscuits and makes them taste even more indulgent. For a warm treat any time, store shaped unbaked scones in the freezer for up to one month and bake them to order.

raspberry hazelnut scones

MAKES 8 SCONES

¾ cup (90 g) sorghum flour

¾ cup (70 g) hazelnut flour

½ cup (50 g) oat flour

¼ cup potato starch

2 teaspoons baking powder

2 tablespoons psyllium husk powder

½ teaspoon kosher salt

⅓ cup granulated sugar

8 tablespoons (1 stick) cold unsalted butter, cut into pieces

1 cup fresh raspberries

1 large egg

⅓ cup cold plain whole-milk yogurt

Sanding sugar, for sprinkling

1 In a large bowl, whisk together the sorghum flour, hazelnut flour, oat flour, potato starch, baking powder, psyllium husk powder, salt, and granulated sugar. Using a pastry blender or two knives, cut the butter into the flour mixture until it has the texture of coarse meal with some larger pea-sized pieces. Add the raspberries and toss gently to combine.

2 In a small bowl, whisk together the egg and the yogurt. Add the yogurt mixture to the flour mixture and mix with a fork until a dough forms. (Don't worry too much if the raspberries break apart a bit—you'll just end up with pretty swirls.) Tip the mixture out onto a parchment-lined baking sheet. Pat the dough into a 4 × 8-inch rectangle. Using a sharp knife, cut the dough into 8 squares. (At this point, you can freeze the scones to bake later. Freeze them on the baking sheet until firm, and then transfer them to a resealable plastic freezer bag.) Spread the squares out evenly on the lined sheet, and put in the freezer for 20 to 30 minutes. Meanwhile, preheat the oven to 400°F.

3 Sprinkle the tops of the scones with sanding sugar. Bake until they are golden brown and a toothpick inserted into the center comes out with moist crumbs attached, 20 to 24 minutes. Serve warm.

tip Bake frozen, shaped scones directly from the freezer. Just be sure to add a few minutes to the baking time.

I have high standards for home fries. I need onions. I crave herbs. I want greens! That's how this dish evolved. These pumped-up hash browns with eggs make a wonderfully rich and satisfying breakfast. Leftovers are just as tasty over some cooked quinoa or brown rice.

sweet potato and spinach hash

SERVES 4

2 medium sweet potatoes (about 9 ounces each), peeled and cut into ½-inch pieces

Kosher salt

2 tablespoons olive oil

1 small onion, halved and thinly sliced

2 garlic cloves, minced

2 cups packed fresh baby spinach

2 teaspoons finely grated lemon zest (see Tip)

4 large eggs

Freshly ground black pepper

2 tablespoons thinly sliced fresh mint leaves

Labneh, homemade (page 26) or store-bought, crème fraîche, or Greek yogurt, for serving (optional)

1 In a 10-inch nonstick skillet, bring ½ cup of water to a boil over medium-high heat. Add the sweet potatoes and ½ teaspoon salt, and cover the skillet. Cook until just tender, stirring occasionally, 4 to 5 minutes. Remove the cover and continue to cook until the water has completely evaporated, 2 to 3 minutes. Transfer the potatoes to a plate and wipe out the skillet with a paper towel.

2 Heat the oil in the skillet over medium heat until hot. Add the onions and garlic and cook, stirring often, until the onions are soft and golden, about 8 minutes. Stir in the potatoes and spread the mixture out in an even layer. Cook without stirring until the potatoes are hot and browned in spots, 3 to 4 minutes. Gently fold in the spinach and lemon zest, and cook just until the spinach is wilted. Season to taste with salt, and transfer the hash to a platter and keep warm.

3 Crack the eggs into the skillet, season with salt and pepper, and cook them to your liking. Top each serving of the hash with a fried egg, some mint, and a few dollops of labneh, if desired.

---

tip Zesting a lemon removes the fruit's protective outer layer and leaves it defenseless against the elements. To keep the fruit fresh, be sure to wrap it tightly in plastic wrap and store it in the fridge.

A few easy extra steps can transform an ordinary breakfast into a luxurious treat. Here the labneh renders the eggs both silky and fluffy, and a quick roast in the oven transforms plum tomatoes into a sweet and tangy accompaniment. The result is a Sunday brunch revelation that is sure to be your new go-to when company comes.

roasted tomatoes with labneh, soft scrambled eggs, and za'atar

SERVES 4

6 plum tomatoes, cut into ¼-inch-thick slices

6 teaspoons olive oil

Kosher salt

6 large eggs

3 tablespoons labneh, homemade (page 26) or store-bought, or sour cream, plus more for serving

Fresh Herb Za'atar (page 22), for sprinkling

1 Preheat the oven to 425°F. In a jelly-roll pan or a large oven-safe skillet, lay the tomato slices cut side down. Drizzle with 4 teaspoons of the oil and lightly sprinkle with salt. Roast until soft and browned in spots, 25 to 30 minutes.

2 When the tomatoes are almost done, whisk together the eggs, labneh, and a light sprinkle of salt in a medium bowl. Heat the remaining 2 teaspoons olive oil in a large nonstick skillet over low heat. Add the egg mixture and cook, stirring constantly, until the eggs are set but still slightly wet, 3 to 4 minutes. (Feel free to cook them longer if you prefer.)

3 Serve the eggs with the tomatoes, a dollop of labneh, and a sprinkling of za'atar.

What better way to eat greens for breakfast than swirled into cheesy grits and topped with a perfectly runny egg? I love smoky, nutty Gouda with the peppery arugula, but feel free to use any cheese you have on hand. Cheddar or Fontina would also be lovely.

smoked gouda grits with eggs and arugula

SERVES 4

1 teaspoon distilled white vinegar

4 large eggs

1 cup whole milk, plus more for serving if desired

1 cup corn grits

½ cup shredded smoked Gouda cheese, plus more for serving if desired

3 cups baby arugula, coarsely chopped

¼ cup fresh cilantro leaves, torn, plus more for serving if desired

1 tablespoon unsalted butter

Kosher salt and freshly ground black pepper

1 Bring 2 to 3 inches of water to a boil in a small saucepan. Add the vinegar and reduce the heat to a low simmer. Crack 1 egg into a small dish. With a wooden spoon, swirl the simmering water to create a little whirlpool. Very gently add the egg to the center of the whirlpool and let it roll around a bit. Once it has slowed down, use a slotted spoon to fold the loose whites up and over the yolk, and then let the egg cook undisturbed for 3 minutes.

2 Carefully lift the egg out with a slotted spoon and set it on a paper-towel-lined plate. Repeat with the remaining eggs. (Give the eggs a quick dip back in the hot water just before serving if desired.)

3 In a medium saucepan, bring the milk and 3 cups of water to a boil. While stirring, add the grits and then reduce the heat to low and simmer. Cook until thickened, stirring occasionally, about 8 minutes.

4 Stir the Gouda, arugula, cilantro, and butter into the grits and cook until the arugula is wilted, 2 to 3 minutes. Add a splash of milk if you like the texture a little looser. Season with salt and pepper to taste. Serve the grits topped with an egg, and with some additional cheese and cilantro if desired.

This is one of the fastest and easiest sweets I've ever created. The batter comes together in one bowl, without the use of any special machinery, and bakes up in minutes—great news for the doughnut-lovers in your house.

spiced doughnuts with mocha glaze

MAKES 6 DOUGHNUTS

BATTER

4 tablespoons (½ stick) unsalted butter, melted and cooled slightly, plus more for the pan

½ cup (45 g) almond flour

½ cup (50 g) oat flour

½ cup granulated sugar

⅓ cup (60 g) potato starch

1 tablespoon psyllium husk powder

¼ teaspoon baking powder

½ teaspoon freshly grated nutmeg

½ teaspoon kosher salt

¼ teaspoon baking soda

1 large egg

¼ cup sour cream

½ teaspoon pure vanilla extract

1 Prepare the batter: Preheat the oven to 350°F. Butter a 6-cup doughnut pan. In a large bowl, whisk together the almond flour, oat flour, granulated sugar, potato starch, psyllium husk powder, baking powder, nutmeg, salt, and baking soda. Add the butter, egg, sour cream, and vanilla, and whisk to combine.

2 Transfer the batter to a resealable plastic bag and cut off one corner to make about a ½-inch opening. Squeeze the batter evenly into the molds of the prepared pan. Bake until a toothpick inserted into a doughnut comes out clean, 10 to 12 minutes. Transfer the pan to a rack to cool slightly; then carefully tip the doughnuts out onto the rack to cool completely.

---

tip I use a Norpro doughnut pan for my baked doughnuts. The deep cavities and tall center posts of the molds create the best-shaped doughnuts around. Just be sure to butter the mold well—a warm doughnut stuck to the pan is a heartbreaking sight.

(RECIPE CONTINUES)

GLAZE

1 teaspoon pure vanilla extract

1 teaspoon instant espresso powder

2 tablespoons unsweetened Dutch-process cocoa powder

½ cup confectioners' sugar

4 teaspoons whole milk, plus more if needed

Sprinkles (optional)

3 Make the glaze: In a shallow bowl, combine the vanilla and espresso powder. Then add the cocoa powder, sugar, and milk, and whisk to make a smooth glaze. Add a little more milk if necessary.

4 Dip the top of each cooled doughnut in the glaze. Top with sprinkles, if desired. Doughnuts are best the day they're made. Store any leftovers in an airtight container at room temperature for up to 3 days.

make every crumb count

Most baked goods are best on the day that they're baked. I find that they rarely last longer than that anyway! But here are a few tips for making the most out of all your hard work so nothing goes to waste.

- Some baked goods can be frozen before baking and then made to order. The Raspberry Hazelnut Scones (page 51) and the cookies for the Oatmeal–Chocolate Chunk Ice Cream Sandwiches (page 187) are perfect for planning ahead!
- Day-old bread makes great breadcrumbs and bread pudding (see page 185). How about crumbling stale Cinnamon Graham Crackers (page 164) over ice cream? Or try making sweet croutons out of the Maple-Glazed Butternut Squash Bread (page 46) to serve with vanilla custard.
- Don't overlook the freezer! Pop a well-wrapped baked good in the freezer and extend its shelf life for at least a month. Stash baked Spiced Doughnuts (page 57) and glaze them just before serving.

Warm brown rice, simmered with milk, is a cozy and filling alternative to oatmeal. Chia are tiny, nutrient-dense seeds from *Salvia hispanica,* a plant native to Mexico and Guatemala. Packed with omega-3 fatty acids, fiber, and protein, they add texture to this creamy breakfast pudding. Or dress it up with in-season berries that you've warmed over the stove for just a few minutes.

breakfast pudding with chia, coconut, and cacao nibs

SERVES 4

1 cup short-grain brown rice

1½ cups whole milk, plus more for serving if desired

1 to 2 tablespoons maple syrup

2 tablespoons chia seeds

2 small bananas, sliced, for serving

Unsweetened coconut flakes, toasted, for serving

Cacao nibs, for serving

1 In a medium saucepan, bring the rice and 2¼ cups of water to a boil. Reduce the heat to maintain a low simmer, cover partially, and cook until the rice is tender and the water has been absorbed, about 30 minutes.

2 Add the milk and bring to a simmer. Add the maple syrup and the chia seeds, and cook until the mixture is thick and creamy, about 2 minutes. (The pudding will continue to thicken as it sits.) Top it with the bananas, coconut, cacao nibs, and more milk if you like.

creamy breakfast
quinoa with roasted
strawberries, page 62

Quinoa makes a surprisingly tasty addition to the breakfast table. In this recipe, I've cooked it down with plenty of milk to make a heavenly alternative to oatmeal. Roasted maple strawberries, with their luscious concentrated juices, take the whole thing to another level—this dish looks and tastes like dessert.

creamy breakfast quinoa with roasted strawberries

SERVES 4

QUINOA

¾ cup quinoa, rinsed and drained

2½ cups whole or 2% milk, plus more for serving

Pinch of kosher salt

STRAWBERRIES

1½ cups fresh strawberries, hulled and quartered (if large)

1 tablespoon maple syrup, plus more for serving

1 tablespoon unsalted butter, cut into pieces

¼ teaspoon ground cinnamon

1 Preheat the oven to 400°F. In a medium saucepan, combine the quinoa, milk, and salt. Simmer over medium heat, partially covered, stirring occasionally, until the mixture has cooked down and thickened slightly and the quinoa is very tender, 25 to 30 minutes.

2 Meanwhile, in a small baking dish, toss the strawberries with the maple syrup, butter, and cinnamon. Bake until the strawberries have softened and released some of their juice, stirring halfway through, about 10 minutes total.

3 Serve the quinoa topped with the roasted strawberries, extra milk, and a drizzle of maple syrup.

Granola might be the most versatile breakfast food around. It is easy to throw together, tastes great, and even makes a lovely gift. Here I add flaxseeds for their pleasant nuttiness and some of those valuable omega-3s. I like this tropical, lime-scented version both on top of plain yogurt in the morning and over vanilla ice cream at night.

coconut-lime granola with cashews

MAKES ABOUT 5 CUPS

4 tablespoons (½ stick) melted unsalted butter or coconut oil

¼ cup maple syrup

4 teaspoons finely grated lime zest (from 1 lime)

¼ teaspoon kosher salt

2 cups old-fashioned rolled oats

½ cup unsweetened flaked coconut

½ cup roasted salted cashews, chopped

¼ cup flaxseed meal

⅓ cup dried fruit, such as sour cherries or golden raisins, chopped

1 Preheat the oven to 350°F. In a large bowl, combine the butter, maple syrup, lime zest, and salt. Add the oats, coconut, and cashews, and stir until everything is well coated. Add the flaxseed meal and toss to combine.

2 Transfer the mixture to a parchment-lined rimmed baking sheet and spread it out over three quarters of the sheet. Bake until the oats and coconut are deep golden and crisp, 30 to 40 minutes, rotating the sheet halfway through. Transfer the sheet to a rack to cool completely.

3 When the sheet is completely cool, use an overturned spatula to scrape under the granola and break it into pieces. Add the dried fruit and toss to combine. Store the granola in an airtight container at room temperature for up to 1 week or in the freezer for up to 1 month.

soups, sides, and salads

For years I worked as a food editor in magazine test kitchens. I loved my job. But there is one thing I gave up as a food editor: lunch. When I was cooking all day, developing recipes, I rarely stopped for a proper lunch. There was never a need—we started most days with food and ate throughout the day. I never minded this luxury, but when I was eating salmon at 9:30 a.m., tasting a half dozen pies by noon, and sampling roast turkey at 4 p.m., I craved a simple, healthy midday meal. Now that I work from home, I'm taking back lunch and I'm enjoying it.

Lunch is an opportunity to eat something wonderful *and* get more hearty vegetables and gluten-free grains into your diet. The dishes in this chapter can be served alone or as accompaniments to a grander meal. Carrots with Miso-Orange Butter (page 83) would be lovely alongside a juicy roast chicken. Roasted Vegetable Salad with Creamy Horseradish Dressing (page 94) would be killer with a couple of grilled rib eye steaks. The French Lentil and Harissa Salad (page 88) and the Red Quinoa and Brussels Sprout Salad (page 86) are perfect for packing for an office lunch or, better yet, a picnic in the park. All of these simple dishes hit the spot when I'm craving comfort. And—let's be honest—when I don't want to wash that many dishes.

This is the kind of soup that could knock out a cold with one bowl. Ginger-infused chicken broth is warming from the inside out, and the spinach, eggs, and brown rice are both filling and nutritious. I like spinach here because it's easy to prep and cooks quickly, but you could use any leafy greens that you prefer.

gingery chicken soup with spinach and eggs

SERVES 4

1 tablespoon olive oil

1 large shallot, thinly sliced

2-inch knob fresh ginger, peeled and cut into matchsticks

4 large garlic cloves, thinly sliced

6 cups chicken broth (page 20)

½ cup short-grain brown rice

5 ounces fresh baby spinach, coarsely chopped

Kosher salt and freshly ground black pepper

4 large eggs

Fresh cilantro leaves, for serving (optional)

1 In a large pot, heat the oil over medium heat. Add the shallots and cook, stirring often, until it is soft and translucent, 4 to 6 minutes. Add the ginger, garlic, chicken broth, and 2 cups of water and bring to a simmer. Add the rice and continue to simmer, partially covered, until the rice is tender, 30 to 35 minutes.

2 Add the spinach and cook just until it is tender, about 2 minutes. Season the soup to taste with salt and pepper. Reduce the heat to a very gentle simmer. Crack one of the eggs into a small bowl and then gently pour it into the soup at the edge of the pot. Repeat this with the remaining eggs.

3 Cook until the egg whites are set and the yolks are still runny, 3 to 5 minutes. To serve, ladle an egg into each bowl and then add the broth, rice, and greens. Top with cilantro leaves, if desired.

Red lentils are a busy cook's best friend. They have a nice way of yielding to broth, becoming tender and creamy without much time or effort. If you can find it, fresh chorizo, as opposed to dried, is a nice addition. The spices are usually a little milder than in the dried sausage and work nicely with the kale and lentils.

kale and red lentil soup

SERVES 4

2 tablespoons olive oil

1 medium onion, cut into small dice

2 large garlic cloves, minced

8 ounces fresh gluten-free chorizo sausage, casings removed (see Tip)

1 large sweet potato (about 14 ounces), peeled and diced

4 cups chicken broth (page 20)

8 ounces Lacinato kale, stemmed and thinly sliced

¾ cup red lentils

1 to 2 tablespoons distilled white vinegar or fresh lemon juice

Kosher salt and freshly ground black pepper

1 In a large heavy-bottomed pot, heat the oil over medium-low heat. Add the onions and garlic and cook, stirring occasionally, until translucent and softened, about 8 minutes.

2 Increase the heat to medium, add the chorizo, and cook, breaking the meat up with a wooden spoon, until it is no longer pink, 2 to 3 minutes. Add the sweet potato and cook for another 2 to 3 minutes.

3 Stir in the chicken broth and 2 cups of water. Bring to a simmer and cook until the potatoes begin to soften, about 10 minutes. Stir in the kale and the lentils, and cook until the lentils are just tender (not mushy), 10 to 15 minutes. Stir in the vinegar, and season with salt and pepper to taste.

tip My grocery store sells fresh chorizo at the butcher counter. Some days the chorizo is perfect and some days the links are like little salt bombs, so I've learned to season with care. Like many dishes, this soup is even better with a dollop of sour cream on top.

This is the kind of smooth, creamy soup that you could drink out of a mug for extra coziness. The gomasio, or sesame salt, is not absolutely necessary, but it adds a pleasant nuttiness. The secret ingredient is miso paste, a salty, super-flavorful Japanese seasoning made from fermented soybeans.

roasted kabocha squash soup with gomasio

SERVES 4 TO 6

1 medium kabocha squash (about 3¼ pounds), halved and seeded

3 tablespoons neutral oil, such as safflower

5 scallions

1 tablespoon minced peeled fresh ginger

4 cups chicken or vegetable broth (pages 20 and 21)

¼ cup gluten-free white miso (see Tip)

Kosher salt

1 tablespoon unseasoned rice vinegar

Gomasio, homemade (page 27) or store-bought, for sprinkling

tip Some varieties of miso include barley, wheat, or rye, so be sure to read the label carefully. Look for gluten-free misos made with rice, buckwheat, or millet.

1 Preheat the oven to 400°F. Drizzle the flesh of the squash halves with 1 tablespoon of the oil, and set them cut side down on a rimmed baking sheet. Bake until the squash is tender when pierced with a knife, about 30 minutes. Let the squash stand until it is cool enough to handle. Then scoop the flesh into a bowl. You should have about 3 cups.

2 Trim and thinly slice the scallions, reserving about ½ cup of the sliced dark green tops for garnish. In a large pot, heat the remaining 2 tablespoons oil over medium heat. Add the scallions and the ginger and cook, stirring occasionally, until softened, about 5 minutes.

3 Add the squash, broth, and 2 cups of water and stir to combine. Cover the pot and bring the mixture to a boil; then reduce to a low simmer. Cook until the liquid has reduced a bit and the soup has thickened, about 20 minutes.

4 In a small bowl, whisk the miso with a bit of the hot soup until smooth. Add the miso mixture to the soup and stir to combine. Season to taste with salt.

5 In batches, transfer the soup to a blender and puree until smooth (being careful when blending hot liquids). Stir in the vinegar and reheat the soup if necessary. Top the soup with the reserved scallion greens and a bit of gomasio before serving.

Millet is a wonderful quick-cooking, gluten-free grain that is a perfect alternative to rice. Here I've made a basic millet pilaf that would be nice served alongside roasted meats or with stews, like the clam and tomato stew on page 104, where it can soak up all the delicious juices. Millet is best served warm the day it's made, as it tends to dry out in the fridge.

basic millet pilaf

SERVES 4

1 tablespoon unsalted butter

1 tablespoon olive oil, plus more for serving if desired

1 small onion, diced

Kosher salt

1 cup millet

3 strips lemon zest

2 sprigs fresh thyme

2 cups chicken or vegetable broth (pages 20 and 21)

½ cup chopped fresh parsley leaves

Fresh lemon juice, for serving

1 In a medium pot, melt the butter with the olive oil over medium heat. Add the onions and a few pinches of salt, and cook, stirring occasionally, until the onions are soft and translucent, 6 to 8 minutes. Add the millet and toast it for a minute or two, stirring. Add the lemon zest strips, thyme sprigs, and broth, and bring to a boil over high heat.

2 Reduce the heat to medium-low to maintain a gentle simmer and cook, covered, until the grains are tender and have absorbed the liquid, about 20 minutes. Remove the pot from the heat and let it stand for 10 minutes.

3 Remove the thyme sprigs and lemon zest. Stir in the parsley and a few squeezes of lemon juice. Season with salt to taste. Drizzle each serving with olive oil, if desired.

These potatoes are so good that they never make it to the table. As soon as they come out of the oven, I stand over the baking sheet in the kitchen and eat them with my fingers like an animal.

SERVES 4 TO 6

1¾ pounds baby Yukon Gold potatoes, scrubbed

Kosher salt

Extra virgin olive oil, for drizzling

1 tablespoon Fresh Herb Za'atar (page 22)

crispy smashed potatoes with fresh herb za'atar

1 Put the potatoes in a large pot and add cold water to cover by 1 inch. Season with salt. Bring to a boil and cook just until the potatoes are fork-tender, 20 minutes. While the potatoes are cooking, preheat the oven to 450°F.

2 Drain the potatoes well and tip them out onto a large rimmed baking sheet. Let them cool slightly. Then, with the palm of your hand, gently flatten each potato. Drizzle them with olive oil and sprinkle with the za'atar and salt to taste. Roast the potatoes until the edges are crisp and brown, 20 to 30 minutes.

I first learned about gently poaching food in olive oil back when I worked at *Fine Cooking*. Food writer Molly Stevens had written an excellent story on the glories of poaching fish in the flavorful oil, and I was smitten: The results were tender and succulent. A real revelation! Since then, I've been olive-oil-poaching anything and everything and have found that vegetables take really well to a warm oil bath. They melt down into a delicious, silky version of their former selves without ever tasting greasy.

braised vegetable ragout

SERVES 4

1 small fennel bulb, halved, cored, and thinly sliced, fronds reserved for garnish

1 small onion, halved and thinly sliced

2 cups cherry tomatoes

4 sprigs fresh thyme

5 garlic cloves, lightly crushed

Kosher salt and freshly ground black pepper

1 cup olive oil

1 Preheat the oven to 325°F. In a 9 × 13-inch baking dish combine the fennel, onions, tomatoes, thyme sprigs, and garlic. Season to taste with salt and pepper. Add the olive oil and toss to make sure the vegetables are well coated in oil.

2 Bake the vegetables until they are very soft and silky, about 1 hour and 30 minutes. To serve, remove the vegetables from the oil and transfer them to a platter. Season to taste with salt and pepper. Garnish with the fennel fronds.

---

tip This recipe calls for fennel and tomatoes (they're a treat to the eye as well as the palate), but this poaching method works with whatever veggies you're craving; try carrots, zucchini, or leeks.

These hot, spicy fritters are sure to please anyone. Bob's Red Mill makes the protein- and fiber-rich garbanzo-fava blend I like. If you can't find it, feel free to use plain chickpea flour, also called besan, as a substitute. Serve the fritters topped with plain Greek yogurt swirled with grated lime zest.

carrot fritters

MAKES ABOUT 12 FRITTERS

3 medium carrots, peeled and shredded (2 cups)

½ small onion, very thinly sliced

1 to 2 serrano chiles, seeded and minced (see Tip, page 23)

3 tablespoons chopped fresh cilantro leaves, plus more for serving

2 large eggs, lightly beaten

1 cup (115 g) garbanzo-fava flour or chickpea flour

½ teaspoon baking powder

Kosher salt

Peanut or vegetable oil, for frying

Lime wedges, for serving

1 Preheat the oven to 200°F. Set a paper-towel-lined baking sheet or an oven-safe plate in the oven. In a large bowl, combine the carrots, onions, chiles, and cilantro. Add the eggs and stir to combine.

2 In a small bowl, whisk together the garbanzo-fava flour, baking powder, and 1½ teaspoons salt. Add the flour mixture to the carrot mixture and stir to combine.

3 In a nonstick skillet, heat about ¼ inch of oil over medium-high heat. When the oil is hot, drop 2-tablespoon scoops of the batter evenly in the pan and then flatten them slightly. Cook until golden brown and cooked through, flipping halfway through, 3 to 4 minutes total.

4 Using a slotted spoon or a fish spatula, transfer the fritters to the prepared baking sheet in the oven. Repeat with the remaining batter. Serve hot with a sprinkle of salt, a wedge of lime, and some cilantro.

Big family meals were my favorite part of our trips to Sri Lanka when I was a kid. The table would be covered with bowls of curries, condiments, and rice, and every seat was filled. On quieter days, dinners were simpler, with less fuss and fanfare but still with plenty of comforting food. This is my version of the stir-fried noodles that we used to eat at my grandmother's house on those nights—a simple dish that came together quickly when we were ravenous.

This recipe starts with the obvious South Asian touches—like fresh curry leaves, cabbage, and coconut oil—but then it veers off a bit with fish sauce and Sriracha. It's not traditional, but I like the way the heat and salt play off the sweetness of the coconut oil. Serve this dish with some sliced skirt steak or a steamed fish to make a hearty dinner. Or skip the meat and use a gluten-free tamari instead of the fish sauce for a vegetarian meal.

stir-fried rice vermicelli

SERVES 4

6 ounces rice vermicelli noodles, roughly broken into 4-inch lengths

¼ cup coconut oil

3 tablespoons minced peeled fresh ginger

4 garlic cloves, minced

10 to 12 fresh curry leaves

4 scallions, trimmed and cut into ¼-inch slices

½ medium head green cabbage, thinly sliced

1 large carrot, peeled and cut into thin matchsticks

2 to 3 tablespoons fish sauce

2 to 3 teaspoons Asian hot sauce, such as Sriracha

1 Cook the rice vermicelli according to the package instructions.

2 While the vermicelli is cooking, heat the oil in a large skillet or wok over medium-high heat. Add the ginger, garlic, curry leaves, and scallions and cook until fragrant and starting to soften, about 3 minutes.

3 Add the cabbage and carrot and cook, stirring often, until softened, 3 to 5 minutes. Add 2 tablespoons of the fish sauce and 2 teaspoons of the hot sauce. Add the drained noodles and toss to combine. Season with additional fish sauce and Sriracha, if desired.

Millet is a flavor sponge. It wants to soak up all the tasty things you can think to throw at it. Here I've studded it with briny green olives and sweet-tart apricots: a classic Moroccan combination that adds a lot of flavor with very little effort.

millet pilaf with apricots, olives, and toasted almonds

SERVES 4

1 tablespoon unsalted butter

1 tablespoon olive oil, plus more for serving if desired

1 small onion, diced

1 cup millet

2 cups chicken broth (page 20)

⅓ cup chopped dried apricots

⅓ cup sliced almonds, toasted

¼ cup sliced pitted green olives

½ cup chopped fresh cilantro leaves

Kosher salt

1 In a medium pot, melt the butter with the olive oil over medium heat. Add the onions and cook until it is soft and translucent, about 5 minutes. Add the millet and toast it for a minute or two, stirring.

2 Add the broth and bring to a boil over high heat. Reduce the heat to medium-low to maintain a gentle simmer and cook, covered, until the grains are tender and have absorbed the liquid, about 20 minutes. Remove the pot from the heat and let it stand for 10 minutes.

3 Stir in the apricots, almonds, olives, and cilantro. Season with salt to taste. Drizzle with olive oil before serving, if desired.

As soon as you get home from the store, cut off the green tops of your baby carrots. Just like a carrot that's still growing in the ground, the leafy greens will continue to pull sweetness from their roots. You'll want to save all that sweetness for this recipe.

carrots with miso-orange butter

SERVES 4

1½ pounds thin carrots, scrubbed

4 teaspoons neutral oil, such as safflower

Kosher salt

2 tablespoons unsalted butter, at room temperature

1 tablespoon gluten-free white miso (see Tip, page 72)

¾ teaspoon finely grated orange zest

1 Preheat the oven to 425°F. On a rimmed baking sheet, toss the carrots with the oil. Season lightly with salt. Roast the carrots until they are tender and browned in spots, flipping them over halfway through, 30 to 35 minutes.

2 Meanwhile, stir together the butter, miso, and orange zest. Top the hot carrots with the miso butter before serving.

Kiribath, or "milk rice," is a beloved Sri Lankan dish. It consists of rice that has been cooked with coconut milk until it becomes a mushy, semi-solid porridge. I've always thought that the flavor was perfect but the texture could use an update. This coconut rice has all the creamy sweetness of *kiribath* but a bit more structure. It pairs nicely with Miso Shrimp with Snap Peas (page 119) and would be delicious served underneath a big scoop of the Black Bean and Tomatillo Chili (page 101).

coconut rice with fried shallots

SERVES 4 TO 6

1¾ cups coconut milk

1½ cups white jasmine or basmati rice

1 teaspoon kosher salt

2 tablespoons coconut oil

2 large shallots, thinly sliced

1 In a medium pot, bring the coconut milk and 1 cup of water to a simmer. Add the rice and salt and cook, partially covered, until the liquid has been almost completely absorbed and the rice is just tender, about 20 minutes. Remove from the heat, cover the pot, and let stand for 5 minutes.

2 Meanwhile, heat the oil in a small saucepan over medium-high heat. Add the shallots and cook, stirring, until golden brown, 4 to 5 minutes. Use a slotted spoon to transfer the shallots to a paper-towel-lined plate. To serve, top the coconut rice with the shallots.

This salad reminds me of the high school romance I always wished I had. Carrots, a veggie superstar, play the part of the popular guy, if you will: easy to love, so sweet and handsome, and everyone knows it. The less popular grassy sorghum, on the other hand, is cool in an understated way once you get to know her. Together they bring out the best in each other. Sweet and earthy with a bit of spice, this pairing has it all.

SERVES 4

1 cup sorghum

4 tablespoons (½ stick) unsalted butter, plus more for serving

Kosher salt

2 teaspoons coriander seeds

3 medium carrots, peeled and shredded

1 small jalapeño chile, seeded and diced (see Tip, page 23)

1 teaspoon finely grated lime zest (from 1 lime)

2 tablespoons fresh lime juice (from 2 limes)

½ cup packed fresh cilantro leaves, chopped

Extra virgin olive oil, for drizzling

¼ cup crumbled soft feta cheese

warm carrot and sorghum salad

1 In a medium saucepan, bring the sorghum, 1 tablespoon of the butter, a generous pinch of salt, and 4 cups of water to a boil. Reduce the heat to a simmer and cook, partially covered, until the liquid has been absorbed and the sorghum is tender, 55 to 65 minutes. If necessary, add more water and cook the sorghum a little longer.

2 In a large skillet, heat the remaining 3 tablespoons butter over medium heat. Add the coriander seeds and cook, stirring occasionally, until fragrant, about 1 minute. Add the carrots and jalapeño and cook until they've just softened, 2 to 4 minutes. Stir in the sorghum, lime zest, and lime juice and cook for another minute or two. Season to taste with salt. Just before serving, stir in the cilantro, drizzle with olive oil, and top with the feta.

Red quinoa makes a grain salad look pretty and taste delicious. It has the same hearty, nutty flavor as white quinoa, but keeps its firmness after cooking and tossing with a dressing. To up the crunch factor, I've added shredded Brussels sprouts and sweet crisp apples.

red quinoa and brussels sprout salad

SERVES 4

DRESSING

¼ cup tahini, homemade (page 31) or store-bought

¼ cup fresh lemon juice

½ cup packed fresh cilantro leaves, plus more for serving if desired

2 small garlic cloves

1 tablespoon olive oil

½ teaspoon sugar or honey

Kosher salt

SALAD

1 cup red quinoa

Pinch of kosher salt

12 ounces Brussels sprouts, trimmed, halved, and very thinly sliced

2 small apples, such as Honeycrisp or Gala, cored and diced

1 Make the dressing: In an upright blender or using an immersion blender in a liquid measuring cup, combine the tahini, lemon juice, cilantro, garlic, olive oil, sugar, and ¼ cup of water. You should have about ½ cup of dressing. Season to taste with salt and set it aside.

2 Prepare the salad: In a small saucepan, bring the quinoa, salt, and ⅔ cup of water to a boil. Reduce the heat to a simmer, cover, and cook until all of the liquid has been absorbed, about 15 minutes. Remove the pan from the heat and let it stand, covered, for 5 minutes. Then, using a fork, fluff the quinoa.

3 To serve, toss the Brussels sprouts, apples, and cooked quinoa with the dressing. Stir in extra cilantro, if you like.

Puy lentils, also known as French lentils, are the prettiest of the bunch. They lose their beautiful blue marbling after cooking but keep their lovely shape, which is a big plus for salad-making. Here I've paired them with smoky, spicy harissa, plenty of fresh herbs, and tangy goat cheese.

french lentil and harissa salad

SERVES 4

¼ cup olive oil, plus more for drizzling

½ cup chopped shallots

2 cups Puy lentils (*lentilles du Puy*)

3½ cups chicken or vegetable broth (pages 20 and 21)

¾ cup fresh cilantro or mint leaves, chopped, plus more for garnish

¼ cup harissa, homemade (page 23) or store-bought

4 tablespoons sesame seeds, toasted (see Tip, page 31)

3 tablespoons red wine vinegar

Kosher salt

½ cup chopped toasted hazelnuts

2 ounces goat cheese, crumbled (about ½ cup)

1 In a medium saucepan, heat 2 tablespoons of the olive oil over medium heat. Add the shallots and cook until golden brown, about 4 minutes.

2 Add the lentils and the broth and bring to a boil over high heat. Reduce the heat to a low simmer and cook until the lentils are tender and have absorbed the broth, 20 to 30 minutes. If the lentils are tender before all the broth has been absorbed, simply drain off the excess liquid. Let the lentils cool to room temperature.

3 Stir the remaining 2 tablespoons olive oil and the cilantro, harissa, 2 tablespoons of the sesame seeds, and the red wine vinegar into the lentils. Season with salt to taste. Transfer the lentils to a serving dish and top them with the remaining 2 tablespoons sesame seeds, the hazelnuts, the goat cheese, and a drizzle of olive oil.

---

tip This great make-ahead salad becomes a filling lunch, especially when topped with a fried egg.

This is the kind of dish that I could eat over and over again. It's easy to make but seems fancy. The pretty orange-streaked spears make an obvious accompaniment to fish, but they also are heaven simply topped with a poached egg.

garlic saffron asparagus

SERVES 4

2 large garlic cloves

⅛ teaspoon crushed saffron threads

Kosher salt

1 pound fresh asparagus, trimmed

2 tablespoons unsalted butter

1 Using a mortar and pestle, mash the garlic, saffron, and a generous pinch of salt to a paste.

2 In a large skillet, bring about ½ inch of water to a simmer over medium heat. Add the asparagus, cover, and cook until the spears are bright green but still crisp, 1 to 2 minutes. Remove the asparagus and dump out the water. Wipe the skillet dry.

3 Melt the butter in the skillet, and then add the garlic paste. Cook, stirring, until the garlic is fragrant, about 30 seconds. Add the asparagus and toss to coat. Immediately transfer the asparagus to a serving dish. Season to taste with salt if necessary.

---

tip Be careful not to overcook the asparagus in the simmering water. You want it to just begin to soften, as it will continue to cook when you remove it from the water.

Oat berries are the whole oat kernel with only the outer hull removed. You'll find them most often labeled "oat groats," but I can't imagine why. "Oat groats" sounds like something a grumpy ogre might dine on. "Oat berries," on the other hand, sounds like the tasty little morsels they are. They cook up chewy and hearty, like farro or brown rice, and make an excellent addition to hearty grain salads.

oat berry salad with cauliflower, dates, and mint

SERVES 4

1 small head cauliflower (1½ pounds), trimmed, cored, and sliced into ½-inch-thick steaks (see Tip)

3 tablespoons olive oil

Kosher salt and freshly ground black pepper

1 cup gluten-free oat berries

1 teaspoon finely grated lemon zest

4 teaspoons fresh lemon juice

2 teaspoons red wine vinegar

4 large dried Medjool dates, pitted and chopped (½ cup; see Tip, page 196)

½ cup chopped fresh mint leaves, plus more for serving

1 Preheat the oven to 400°F. Lay the cauliflower slices in a single layer on a rimmed baking sheet. Drizzle with 2 tablespoons of the olive oil and toss them gently to coat both sides. Season to taste with salt and pepper. Roast the cauliflower until tender and golden brown in spots, 30 to 40 minutes, flipping halfway through.

2 Meanwhile, in a medium saucepan, combine the oat berries with 2 cups of water and bring to a boil over high heat. Reduce the heat to a gentle simmer and cook, partially covered, until the oat berries are tender and the liquid has been absorbed, 25 to 35 minutes.

3 Cut the cauliflower into 1- to 2-inch pieces. In a large bowl, whisk together the lemon zest, lemon juice, red wine vinegar, and remaining tablespoon of olive oil. Add the oat berries, cauliflower, dates, and mint, and toss well to combine. Season to taste with salt and pepper. Serve warm or at room temperature, topped with more mint.

tip Instead of breaking cauliflower into florets, slice the head into big, flat steaks before roasting. That way, as much surface area as possible touches the pan and you get more caramelized-vegetable goodness to enjoy.

This salad is simple, but it has the power to change hearts and minds. One of my favorite "beetophobes," my friend Merritt, also claimed to dislike horseradish. Double whammy! I gave her this recipe to try and she complied dutifully. She loved it so much that she found herself slathering the leftover sauce on sandwiches the next day. And guess what? She's even Team Beets now!

roasted vegetable salad with creamy horseradish dressing

SERVES 4

2 medium fennel bulbs, halved, cored, and sliced ¼ inch thick, fronds reserved for garnish

2 tablespoons olive oil, plus more for drizzling

Kosher salt and freshly ground black pepper

6 medium beets, trimmed and scrubbed

⅔ cup labneh, homemade (page 26) or store-bought, or sour cream

2 teaspoons freshly grated horseradish, or 4 teaspoons prepared horseradish

2 teaspoons fresh lime juice (from 1 lime)

½ cup pistachios, toasted and coarsely chopped

Finely grated lime zest, for sprinkling

1 Preheat the oven to 425°F. On half of a rimmed baking sheet, toss the fennel with half of the olive oil, season it with salt and pepper, and spread it out in an even layer. On the other half, rub the beets with the remaining oil. Roast until the fennel is tender and browned in spots, about 35 minutes. Transfer the fennel to a plate. Continue to roast the beets until they are tender enough to be pierced with a knife, about 10 minutes more.

2 Let the beets stand until they are cool enough to handle, and then peel off the skin. Slice the beets into ¼-inch-thick slices.

3 In a small bowl, combine the labneh, horseradish, and lime juice. Season to taste with salt and pepper.

4 Arrange the beets and fennel on a platter, and sprinkle with the pistachios, lime zest, fennel fronds, and salt and pepper. Drizzle with more olive oil. Serve with the horseradish dressing on the side.

hearty mains

To me, the perfect gluten-free dinner would require no mention that it's free of gluten. Everyone would be too busy remarking on how tasty it is that you would feel no need to explain or apologize. Silence would be okay, too: the result of food so deeply satisfying that no one stops to say a word. In my family, some people avoid gluten while others don't. I'm sure that's a common scenario in other families, too. I've had to figure out how to make a tasty meal that meets all needs, without anyone feeling deprived or restricted. Over time I've realized how easy this is—even without relying on store-bought gluten-free convenience foods. A delicious naturally gluten-free dinner is simple to make out of hearty grains, meats, and vegetables.

This chapter is full of dinner options—straightforward, delicious meals that are easy to prepare. I like to round out any healthy gluten-free entrée with rice, rice noodles, quinoa, or millet and plenty of vegetables.

Of course, a little extra effort and a few specialty ingredients go a long way in creating pastas, pastry crusts, and other favorite comfort foods. Try the Amaranth Tart with Kale, Caramelized Onions, and Gruyère (page 112) or the Italian-Style Chickpea Socca (page 137) when you have hungry friends over. When the mood for pasta strikes, I've got you covered with Sautéed Lemony Gnocchi (page 131) or Sweet Pea and Ricotta Ravioli (page 142).

These lettuce cups are a riff on one of my favorite recipes of all time: Sesame Steak Salad with Asian Pears, created by my friend (and former boss) Jennifer Armentrout for *Fine Cooking*. I styled the salad for a photograph and could barely keep from eating the flavorful pieces of steak off the plate as we shot it. For this recipe, I've played around with the same flavors wrapped in fun-to-eat lettuce cups with plenty of hearty brown rice, and with a bright hot vinegar sauce drizzled on top.

marinated beef lettuce cups

SERVES 4

BEEF

1 Asian pear, cored and cut into small dice

¼ cup minced peeled fresh ginger

4 garlic cloves, minced

1 serrano chile, seeded and diced (see Tip, page 23)

2 tablespoons fish sauce

1 tablespoon mirin

1 tablespoon gluten-free tamari

1 tablespoon toasted sesame oil

1 tablespoon fresh lemon juice

1½ pounds boneless beef strip steak, thinly sliced against the grain into 2-inch pieces

1 to 2 tablespoons vegetable oil

Kosher salt

SAUCE

2 scallions, trimmed and thinly sliced

2 serrano chiles, thinly sliced (discard the ribs and seeds for less heat)

3 tablespoons distilled white vinegar

2 tablespoons mirin

1 tablespoon gluten-free tamari

1 Prepare the beef: In a blender or with an immersion blender in a bowl, combine the pear, ginger, garlic, chile, fish sauce, mirin, tamari, sesame oil, and lemon juice and blend until well combined.

2 Transfer the marinade to a bowl, add the steak slices, and stir to combine. Cover and refrigerate for 2 to 4 hours.

3 Make the sauce: About 30 minutes before serving, combine the scallions, chiles, vinegar, mirin, and tamari in a small bowl and set aside.

(RECIPE CONTINUES)

2 heads Boston lettuce,
separated into leaves

2 cups cooked short-grain brown rice

1 Asian pear, cored and cut into
small dice

1 small cucumber, peeled, seeded,
and cut into small dice

2 tablespoons sesame seeds, toasted
(see Tip, page 31)

Fish sauce, for drizzling (optional)

4 Remove the steak slices from the marinade and pat them dry.
Heat 1 tablespoon of the oil in a large cast-iron or nonstick
skillet over high heat. Add half of the steak slices in a single
layer, season lightly with salt, and cook until browned in spots
and just cooked through, flipping them over halfway through,
2 to 4 minutes total. With a slotted spoon, transfer the steak to a
plate. Wipe out the skillet, add more oil if necessary, and repeat
with the remaining steak slices.

5 To serve, stuff the lettuce leaves with rice and steak. Top with
the pear, cucumber, and sesame seeds. Drizzle with the vinegar
sauce, and with fish sauce if you like.

This chili tastes even better after a day or two, so make this hearty dish ahead of time and feed your friends and family for days. In this recipe, I cook the tomatillos separately to make sure the acid doesn't stop the beans from getting nice and tender. If you have a little extra time, Spicy Baked Tortilla Chips (page 154) make a lovely addition, crumbled on top.

black bean and tomatillo chili

SERVES 4

2 cups dried black beans

Kosher salt

5 tablespoons vegetable oil

1 medium red onion, diced

5 garlic cloves, minced

1 jalapeño chile, seeded and diced (see Tip, page 23)

1 poblano chile, seeded and diced

3 tablespoons chili powder

1 tablespoon ground cumin

2 fresh bay leaves (or 4 dried leaves)

1 pound tomatillos, peeled, washed, and quartered

Cooked rice, for serving

Tortilla chips (see page 154)

Sliced radishes

Sour cream

Grated cheese, such as cheddar or Monterey Jack

Fresh cilantro leaves

1 The night before you plan to make the chili, soak the beans in a bowl with enough water to cover them and a generous pinch of kosher salt.

2 The next day, drain the beans. Preheat the oven to 325°F. In a medium oven-safe pot, heat 4 tablespoons of the oil over medium heat. Add the onions, garlic, jalapeño, and poblano and cook, stirring occasionally, until the vegetables are soft and the onions are translucent, about 10 minutes. Add the chili powder and cumin and cook, stirring, for 3 minutes. Add the beans, bay leaves, and 4 cups of water. Bring the mixture to a boil; then cover the pot and transfer it to the oven. Bake for 1 hour.

3 Meanwhile, spread the tomatillos on a rimmed baking sheet and toss them with the remaining tablespoon of oil. Set the sheet on an oven rack below the pot of chili and cook until softened and browned in spots, about 1 hour and 15 minutes.

4 After the beans have baked for about an hour, they should be soft. Remove the lid from the pot and continue to bake until the liquid has reduced, about 30 minutes.

5 Transfer the tomatillos to a cutting board and finely chop them. Stir the tomatillos into the chili, remove the bay leaves, and season to taste with salt. Serve over the rice, with the toppings alongside.

In the summer, this dish is on regular rotation in my house; it's a perfect quick meal for those days when you can't bear to stand over a hot stove. My friend Deborah has a gorgeous garden where fresh herbs grow so lushly that I'm practically doing her a favor when I cut them. She grows lovage, too, which is my most beloved herb, and I look forward to using it in this dish all year long. Serve the salmon with some wild rice or millet.

SERVES 4

1¼ pounds boneless, skinless salmon fillet, at least 1 inch thick (see Tip)

¼ cup mixed chopped fresh tender herbs, such as lovage, tarragon, parsley, and dill

2 tablespoons sour cream or crème fraîche

4 teaspoons gluten-free Dijon mustard

Kosher salt and freshly ground black pepper

broiled salmon with herbs and mustard

1 Preheat the broiler with a rack placed 8 inches away from the heat source. Line a rimmed baking sheet with aluminum foil. Set the salmon on the foil.

2 In a small bowl, stir together the herbs, sour cream, mustard, and salt and pepper to taste. Spread the mixture all over the top and sides of the salmon fillet.

3 Broil the salmon until the sauce is browned in spots and the fish is cooked to your liking, 4 to 6 minutes for medium-rare.

tip Make sure to buy a nice thick piece of salmon so that it doesn't overcook under the broiler.

Clams seem like the stuff of fancy Italian restaurants, but once you cook them at home you'll be hooked. Unlike mussels, there is no pesky beard to wrestle with, and they take only a few minutes to cook, creating their own delicious sauce as they simmer. Add a few extras like saffron, tomatoes, and jalapeños, and you'll have a delicious stew to be proud of. I like to serve this with the Basic Millet Pilaf (page 73) or polenta.

saffron-scented clam and tomato stew

SERVES 4

2 tablespoons olive oil

4 garlic cloves, thinly sliced

⅛ teaspoon saffron threads, crushed

3 cups cherry tomatoes, halved

Kosher salt

¼ cup dry white wine

4 pounds littleneck clams, scrubbed

1 jalapeño chile, thinly sliced (remove the ribs and seeds for less heat; see Tip, page 23)

Fresh parsley leaves, for sprinkling (optional)

1 In a large pot, heat the oil over medium heat. Add the garlic and saffron and cook until the garlic is tender and golden, 2 to 3 minutes. Add the tomatoes, season them lightly with salt, and cook until they release their juices and collapse, 2 to 4 minutes.

2 Add the wine and simmer, stirring occasionally, until it has mostly evaporated, 3 to 5 minutes.

3 Add the clams, cover the pot, and cook until they've opened, 8 to 10 minutes, stirring them halfway through. Stir in the jalapeño and the parsley if using, and serve.

This is a rich, satisfying dish that takes very little work and only a touch of planning. All you have to do is remember to soak the beans the night before. Then you can just relax while this cozy stew simmers on the stovetop.

chicken and white bean stew with gremolata

STEW

1½ cups dried cannellini beans

Kosher salt

3 tablespoons olive oil

1 medium onion, finely chopped

1 piece Parmigiano-Reggiano rind (1¾ ounces)

3 small fresh bay leaves (or 6 dried leaves)

6 cups chicken broth (page 20)

2 small boneless, skinless chicken breasts (8 ounces), cut into 4 pieces

¼ cup long-grain white rice, such as jasmine or Carolina

Freshly ground black pepper

GREMOLATA

2 lemons

2 small garlic cloves, crushed through a press

½ cup fresh parsley leaves, finely chopped

½ cup fresh mint leaves

1 Prepare the stew: The night before you plan to make the stew, soak the beans in a bowl with enough water to cover them and a generous pinch of kosher salt.

2 The next day, drain the beans. In a large pot, heat the oil over medium heat. When it is hot, add the onions and cook, stirring occasionally, until it is translucent, 8 to 10 minutes. Add the beans, the Parmigiano rind, the bay leaves, the broth, and 2 cups of water. Bring to a boil over high heat. Then reduce the heat to a gentle simmer and cook until the beans are just tender, 25 to 35 minutes.

3 Stir in the chicken and the rice and cook, uncovered, until the chicken is just cooked through and the rice is tender, 8 to 10 minutes. Transfer the chicken to a cutting board and dice it. Return the diced chicken to the pot. Season the stew with salt and pepper.

4 Make the gremolata: Zest the lemons over a small bowl. Stir in the garlic and the parsley. Just before serving, finely chop the mint and stir it in.

5 Discard the rind and bay leaves, then ladle the stew into individual bowls, sprinkle with the gremolata, and serve.

Chicken and rice is a world-renowned dish. Every culture seems to have its own version. And it's no wonder! Something magical happens when the two cook together. It's as if the very essence of chicken cooks into each grain of rice, rendering it savory and irresistible. Dressed up with silky leeks, plenty of garlic, and sweet, chewy golden raisins, this dish is sure to please.

one-pot chicken thighs with wild rice and leeks

SERVES 4 TO 6

2 tablespoons olive oil

6 bone-in, skin-on chicken thighs (about 6 ounces each)

4 small leeks, light green and white parts thinly sliced (see How to Clean Leeks, opposite)

6 garlic cloves, thinly sliced

¼ cup dry white wine

¾ cup wild rice blend

2 teaspoons chopped fresh thyme leaves

1¾ cups chicken broth (page 20)

¾ cup jasmine rice

¼ cup chopped golden raisins

Kosher salt and freshly ground black pepper

Lemon wedges, for serving

Sour cream, for serving

1 In a 12-inch straight-sided oven-safe skillet, heat the oil over medium-high heat. When the oil is hot, add the chicken thighs, skin side down, and cook until the skin is deep golden brown, 8 to 10 minutes. Transfer the chicken to a plate, skin side up, cover, and set aside. Pour off all except for 2 tablespoons of the fat in the pan.

2 Reduce the heat to medium and add the leeks and garlic to the skillet. Cook, stirring, until the leeks begin to soften and turn golden, 3 to 6 minutes. Add the white wine and cook until the liquid has evaporated. Stir in the wild rice blend, thyme, and chicken broth and bring to a boil over high heat. Reduce to a low simmer, cover, and cook for 25 minutes. Meanwhile, preheat the oven to 350°F.

3 Add the jasmine rice, raisins, ½ teaspoon salt, ¼ teaspoon pepper, and 1¼ cups of water to the skillet, and bring the mixture back to a boil. Return the thighs to the skillet, skin side up, cover the skillet, and transfer it to the oven. Cook until the chicken is cooked through and the rice is almost tender, about 25 minutes. Then remove the lid and cook for another 10 minutes. Let stand for 5 minutes before serving with lemon wedges and dollops of sour cream.

how to clean leeks

Slice the leeks and place them in a bowl of cool water. Swish them around to wash thoroughly, and then lift them out of the water with your hands and set them on a clean plate. Discard the water and the accumulated dirt. Repeat this process until the water is clear. Shake them dry (any extra water will cook off).

Made wholesome with brown rice and quinoa and flavored with sausage, fennel, and a touch of orange zest, this hearty stuffing is wonderful. The bread-based stuffing seems stale in comparison. It's simple enough for Sunday supper but could be a lovely centerpiece of a gluten-free holiday meal. I like to cook the stuffing inside the bird to infuse it with a bit more of that lovely chicken flavor, but it makes a nice dish on its own.

roast chicken with whole-grain sausage stuffing

SERVES 4 TO 6

2 tablespoons olive oil

1 large shallot, finely chopped

1 cup short- or long-grain brown rice

2 cups chicken broth (page 20)

½ cup quinoa, rinsed

1 small fennel bulb (13 ounces), halved, cored, and cut into small dice (1¼ cups)

4 ounces gluten-free hot Italian sausage (about 1 link), casing removed

½ cup chopped fresh parsley leaves

½ teaspoon finely grated orange zest

Kosher salt and freshly ground black pepper

One 3½- to 4-pound whole chicken, patted dry

1 tablespoon unsalted butter, at room temperature

1 In a 10-inch skillet, heat 1 tablespoon of the oil over medium heat. Add the shallots and cook, stirring occasionally, until translucent, about 5 minutes. Add the brown rice and cook until lightly toasted, about 2 minutes. Add the broth and bring to a boil. Reduce the heat to a simmer, cover the skillet, and cook until the rice is almost tender, 20 minutes. Stir in the quinoa and cook, covered, until the liquid has been absorbed and both the rice and the quinoa are tender, another 10 to 15 minutes.

2 Preheat the oven to 425°F. While the oven is heating, heat the remaining 1 tablespoon oil in a 10-inch oven-safe skillet over medium heat. Add the fennel and cook, stirring, until it begins to soften, 4 to 6 minutes. Add the sausage meat and cook until it is no longer pink, breaking it into small pieces as it cooks. Add the rice mixture and cook for a minute or two to meld the flavors. Stir in the parsley and the orange zest. Season to taste with salt and pepper. (Take care with the seasoning: depending on the sausage, you may not need to add much.) Transfer the stuffing mixture to a medium bowl.

3 Set the chicken in the same skillet and use a spoon to fill the cavity loosely with the stuffing. (Any extra stuffing can be served on the side.) Tie the legs together with butcher's twine. Rub the chicken all over with the butter, and season with salt and pepper.

4 Roast the stuffed chicken until a thermometer inserted into the thickest part of a thigh and into the center of the stuffing registers 165°F, 65 to 75 minutes. Cover the chicken with foil if the top gets too brown while it is roasting. Transfer the chicken to a cutting board and let it rest for 10 minutes before carving. Serve the stuffing alongside the chicken. (If the chicken is done before your stuffing reaches the correct temperature, remove the stuffing from the cavity while the chicken is resting and bake it separately in the skillet for a few minutes longer.)

Vinegar, garlic, and plenty of black pepper come together to make a simple version of Filipino adobo sauce. The salty, tangy bite of the sauce is perfect for the mild tofu. Tamari is a rich, dark Japanese soy sauce that is made as a by-product of miso paste. It is usually gluten-free, as opposed to soy sauce, which contains wheat, but always check the label to be safe.

tofu adobo

SERVES 4

1 14-ounce package extra-firm tofu, cut into ½-inch-thick slices

1½ teaspoons cornstarch

2 tablespoons plus 2 teaspoons coconut oil

6 garlic cloves, minced

4 scallions, white and light green parts thinly sliced, dark green slices reserved for garnish

½ cup reduced-sodium gluten-free tamari

⅓ cup distilled white vinegar

3 fresh bay leaves (or 6 dried leaves)

2 teaspoons freshly cracked peppercorns (see Tip)

1½ teaspoons light or dark brown sugar

Cooked rice, for serving

tip You can use a mortar and pestle to crack the peppercorns. Or place the peppercorns between two sheets of parchment and apply pressure with a heavy skillet.

1 Line a rimmed baking sheet with a couple of layers of paper towels. Add the sliced tofu, and then cover it with more paper towels and another baking sheet. Top the baking sheet with a couple of cans. (The added pressure from the cans will help remove extra moisture from the tofu.) Let the tofu stand for 30 minutes.

2 Cut the tofu into ½-inch cubes and toss them with the cornstarch in a medium bowl. Heat 1 tablespoon of the oil in a 10-inch nonstick skillet over high heat. Add half of the tofu, shaking off any excess cornstarch, and cook, undisturbed, until golden brown on one side, 2 to 4 minutes. Flip the tofu over and continue to cook until golden on the other side. Transfer to a clean plate. Repeat with another tablespoon of the oil and the remaining tofu, being sure to shake off the excess cornstarch with each batch.

3 Wipe the skillet clean. Add the remaining 2 teaspoons oil and heat it over medium-high heat. Add the garlic and the white and light green sliced scallions and cook, stirring, until translucent, about 4 minutes. Add the tamari, vinegar, bay leaves, peppercorns, brown sugar, and ¼ cup of water. Bring the mixture to a simmer, cover the skillet, and cook until the scallions are tender and the flavors have melded, about 4 minutes. Return the tofu to the skillet and cook for another 2 minutes, stirring, to warm the tofu and thicken the sauce slightly. Remove the bay leaves and serve the tofu with the rice, topped with the reserved dark green scallions.

Plum tomatoes were made for sauce. They cook down into the most flavorful marinara—plus, they're cheap and plentiful to boot! But to make a really stellar sauce, you have to blanch them first to remove the skin, which is a tedious process. Here's a way to cheat: Cut out the tough stem bit and halve each tomato crosswise, then roast them, cut side down. The skins shrivel up and you can easily pick them off with a fork. Roasting the tomatoes also concentrates their flavor, making this sauce both easy to make and delicious.

simmered halibut in a roasted tomato sauce

SERVES 4

¼ cup olive oil

4 garlic cloves, thinly sliced

2 canned anchovy fillets

1 large shallot, thinly sliced

3 tablespoons capers

¼ teaspoon Aleppo or red pepper flakes

2 pounds plum tomatoes, stem end cored and halved crosswise

4 skinless halibut fillets (4 to 6 ounces each), bones removed

Kosher salt

1 Preheat the oven to 400°F. In a 12-inch oven-safe skillet, heat the oil, garlic, anchovies, shallots, capers, and pepper flakes over medium heat. Cook, breaking the anchovies up with a wooden spoon, until the shallots are translucent, about 5 minutes.

2 Add the tomatoes, cut side down. Transfer the skillet to the oven and bake until the tomato flesh is very tender and the skins are papery, 45 to 55 minutes.

3 Carefully remove the skillet from the oven and, using a fork, lift out all of the tomato skins and discard them. Stir and mash the tomatoes with a fork. Season the halibut fillets with salt and carefully add them to the sauce. Cover the skillet and return it to the oven. Cook until the fish is opaque throughout, 10 to 15 minutes.

tip In this recipe, I've simmered some fish right in the skillet for a light one-pot dinner. But you could serve the sauce, with or without the fish, over the Sautéed Lemony Gnocchi on page 131 or over a big bowl of creamy polenta.

Amaranth flour is an excellent substitute for wheat flour in pastry. It requires a gentle hand when rolling and shaping, but it bakes into a tender crust that has a lot to offer in both flavor and nutrition. Gooey Gruyère, creamy beans, hearty kale, and soft caramelized onions make this a rich and satisfying meal. Serve fat wedges alongside a simple green salad with a lemony vinaigrette.

amaranth tart with kale, caramelized onions, and gruyère

SERVES 6

DOUGH

¾ cup (80 g) amaranth flour

¾ cup (105 g) brown rice flour

½ cup (90 g) potato starch

1 teaspoon kosher salt

8 tablespoons (1 stick) cold unsalted butter, cut into pieces

FILLING

1 tablespoon olive oil

1 tablespoon unsalted butter

1 large red onion, halved and thinly sliced

Kosher salt and freshly ground black pepper

2 tablespoons dry white wine

3 cups stemmed and coarsely chopped Lacinato kale

1 teaspoon chopped fresh rosemary leaves

2½ cups cooked cannellini beans (see Tip)

4 ounces Gruyère cheese, grated (about 1 cup)

tip This recipe works well with both home-cooked beans (see page 30) and canned beans that have been rinsed and drained.

1 Make the dough: In the bowl of a food processor, combine the amaranth flour, brown rice flour, potato starch, and salt. Add the butter and pulse until combined. Add 6 tablespoons of water and pulse until a dough forms. Add up to 2 tablespoons more water if necessary, but be careful not to make the dough too wet.

2 Tip the dough out onto a sheet of parchment. Cover it with another piece of parchment and roll the dough to form an 11- to 12-inch round. Peel the top parchment off the dough and then flip it over onto a 10-inch tart pan with a removable bottom. Press the dough into the bottom and edges of the pan, and then trim any excess. Patch any cracks with extra dough. Set the pan on a baking sheet and freeze until the dough is firm, 30 minutes. Meanwhile, preheat the oven to 425°F.

3 Line the chilled tart shell with a piece of parchment and fill it with pie weights. Set it on a baking sheet and transfer it to the oven. Bake until the edges are starting to brown and the bottom crust is dry, about 15 minutes. Remove the weights and bake until the crust is golden brown, 10 to 15 minutes.

4 Meanwhile, prepare the filling: In a 10-inch nonstick skillet, heat the oil and butter over medium-low heat. Add the onion slices, season with salt and pepper, and cook, stirring occasionally, until they are soft and caramelized, about 20 minutes. Add the wine and cook until it has evaporated, about 4 minutes. Add the kale and sauté until it is soft, about 5 minutes. Add the rosemary and the beans, and cook until the beans are warmed through and the rosemary is fragrant, about 5 minutes. Adjust the seasoning as necessary.

5 Sprinkle the crust with half of the cheese, add the vegetable mixture, and top with the remaining cheese. Bake just until the cheese has melted, 3 to 5 minutes. Serve hot.

tip Heads-up: This recipe needs to be prepped a day in advance. While you might be tempted to, don't cheat by using canned chickpeas. They are too soft and will make mushy cakes.

I'm lucky enough to live between a Middle Eastern restaurant and a popular falafel takeout joint. Both always emit the most amazing smells—and inspired these chickpea cakes, which are falafel's simpler cousin. Make these cakes vegan by omitting the egg. They will be ever-so-slightly crumblier but still tasty.

green chickpea cakes

SERVES 4

1 cup dried chickpeas

6 tablespoons olive oil

4 whole scallions, trimmed and thinly sliced

4 garlic cloves, thinly sliced

1 cup lightly packed fresh parsley leaves

1 cup lightly packed fresh cilantro leaves

1 cup lightly packed fresh mint leaves

¼ cup tahini, homemade (page 31) or store-bought

2 tablespoons finely grated lemon zest (from 2 lemons)

Kosher salt and freshly ground black pepper

1 large egg

Flaky salt, for serving

Lemon wedges, for serving

Labneh, homemade (page 26) or store-bought, or Greek yogurt, for serving

1 Put the chickpeas in a large bowl and add enough water to cover them by 3 inches. Refrigerate for at least 12 hours and up to 24 hours.

2 Drain the chickpeas and put them in the bowl of a food processor fitted with the metal blade. In a 10-inch nonstick skillet, heat 4 tablespoons of the oil over medium heat. Add the scallions and garlic and cook until just tender, 2 to 4 minutes. Add this mixture to the food processor along with the parsley, cilantro, mint, tahini, and lemon zest. Blend until a sticky, almost smooth paste forms. Season this mixture with salt and pepper to taste. Add the egg and pulse to combine.

3 Transfer the mixture to a bowl, and shape it into 8 patties, about ½ inch thick.

4 Heat 1 tablespoon of the remaining oil in the skillet over medium-high heat. When it is hot, add half of the patties and cook until golden and set on the bottom, about 3 minutes. Carefully flip the patties over and cook until the other side is golden, about 2 minutes. Adjust the heat as necessary to keep the patties from getting too dark before they're cooked through. Transfer the patties to a plate and keep warm. Repeat with the remaining tablespoon of oil and the remaining patties.

5 Sprinkle the patties with flaky salt, and serve with lemon wedges and labneh alongside.

I tested this recipe out on a group of friends on a cold Sunday night. As one of them savored a bite of the juicy chop, she asked, "What did you put on this pork?" I told her the truth. It was nothing brilliant or unique—just plenty of smashed garlic, salt, and pepper. The secret is to start with really nice meat and add a mix of earthy sunchokes, briny olives, and tart preserved lemon, ingredients that make a super-simple meal taste fancy.

garlicky pork chops with roasted sunchokes

SERVES 4

1¼ pounds sunchokes (Jerusalem artichokes), scrubbed and thinly sliced

½ cup sliced pitted green olives

3 tablespoons chopped preserved lemon, homemade (page 25) or store-bought

3 tablespoons plus 2 teaspoons olive oil

Kosher salt and freshly ground black pepper

4 medium garlic cloves, minced

4 bone-in 1-inch-thick pork chops (8 to 9 ounces each; see Tip)

¼ cup chopped fresh parsley leaves

tip If you remember, rub the chops with the garlic mixture in the morning and let them marinate in the fridge all day before you cook them.

1 Preheat the oven to 450°F. In a 9 × 13-inch baking pan, toss together the sunchokes, olives, preserved lemon, and 2 tablespoons of the olive oil. Season with salt and pepper. Roast until the sunchokes are tender and browned in spots, tossing halfway through, 25 to 35 minutes.

2 Meanwhile, using the flat side of a chef's knife or a mortar and pestle, mash the garlic with some salt until you have a paste. Combine the garlic paste with the 2 teaspoons olive oil. Rub the garlic mixture all over the pork chops and set them on a plate. (You can do this step ahead of time to let the flavor penetrate.)

3 Transfer the sunchoke mixture to a serving platter, toss with the parsley, and keep warm.

4 Heat the remaining tablespoon of oil in a large cast-iron skillet over medium-high heat. Season the chops with a bit more salt and pepper, and add them to the skillet. Cook the chops, adjusting the heat as necessary, until they are well browned on both sides and cooked through, 6 to 8 minutes total. A thermometer inserted into the center should read 145°F. (I like my pork chops with a slightly rosy center, but you can cook them longer if you like.) Let the chops rest for a few minutes before serving with the vegetables.

Treat sweet carrots and leeks with a bit of care and they'll reward you with gorgeous complexity. With some stirring and a bit of love, they cook down in this recipe to make a luscious earthy risotto fit for a Sunday dinner. Short-grain brown rice gives the dish a little more heft and a pleasant chewiness.

leek and carrot brown rice risotto

SERVES 4

1½ cups short-grain brown rice

5 cups chicken broth (page 20)

2 tablespoons olive oil

2 medium leeks, light green and white parts thinly sliced (see How to Clean Leeks, page 107)

2 medium carrots, peeled and grated

4 sprigs fresh thyme

Kosher salt and freshly ground black pepper

¼ cup dry white wine

2 tablespoons unsalted butter

½ cup freshly grated Pecorino Romano cheese, plus more for serving

1 In a medium pot, bring the rice and 2 cups of the broth to a simmer. Cover and cook until the rice is partially tender and the liquid has been absorbed, about 20 minutes.

2 Meanwhile, in a small pot, bring the remaining 3 cups broth and 1 cup of water to a low simmer.

3 Transfer the rice to a bowl. Heat the oil in the same pot over medium heat. When it is hot, add the leeks and cook until they are translucent, about 8 minutes. Add the carrots and the thyme sprigs and cook until the carrots begin to soften, about 2 minutes. Season the mixture lightly with salt and pepper. Return the rice to the pot and stir to combine. Add the wine and cook, stirring often, until it is completely absorbed, 1 to 2 minutes.

4 Gradually add the simmering broth, about ½ cup at a time, stirring the mixture until the liquid has been absorbed before adding more. Continue until the rice is tender and the mixture is creamy (you may not need all of the broth). Stir in the butter and the cheese, and season with salt and pepper to taste. Pull out the thyme stems before serving, with extra grated cheese alongside.

Wild lime leaves are bright green and full of flavor. They taste of citrus, but they also have a distinct floral note all their own. A crushed lime leaf is one of the most heavenly aromas on the planet. They can be tricky to find, but your local Asian market is a good bet (if you can't find them, grated lime zest will work in a pinch). Store the leaves in the fridge in an airtight resealable plastic bag for about a week, or in the freezer for longer.

miso shrimp with snap peas

SERVES 4

2 tablespoons neutral oil, such as safflower

6 fresh wild lime leaves, very thinly sliced

2 tablespoons minced peeled fresh ginger

3 tablespoons gluten-free white miso (see Tip, page 72)

1 teaspoon dark or light brown sugar

1 small fresh Thai bird chile, thinly sliced (see Tip, page 23)

8 ounces snow peas, trimmed

1 pound large shrimp, peeled and deveined, cut in half lengthwise

Kosher salt

Cooked buckwheat soba, rice noodles, or brown rice, for serving

1 In a large skillet or wok, heat the oil over medium-high heat. Add the lime leaves and ginger and cook, stirring, until fragrant, 1 to 2 minutes.

2 Add the miso, brown sugar, and chile and toss to combine. Add the snow peas and cook, stirring constantly, for 1 minute.

3 Add the shrimp and cook, stirring, until they are cooked through, 2 to 3 minutes. Season with salt to taste. Serve hot with soba, rice noodles, or rice.

tip A lemongrass stalk adds flavor to stocks, soups, and curries. For this recipe, use only the bottom 4 inches: cut off the bottom, peel off and discard any dry outer layers to get to the tender bulb, trim it to 4 inches, and proceed with the recipe.

I like to serve these fragrant meatballs on top of a big bowl of Coconut Rice with Fried Shallots (page 84) with some freshly grated vegetables. They also make great party appetizers. If ground pork isn't your thing, ground chicken makes a nice substitute; just be sure to buy a combination of both light and dark meat.

lemongrass pork meatballs

SERVES 4

MEATBALLS

1 lemongrass bulb, bottom and tough outer layers removed (see Tip), finely minced

4 teaspoons minced peeled fresh ginger

2 garlic cloves, minced

3 scallions, trimmed

2 teaspoons cornstarch

½ teaspoon dark brown sugar or palm sugar

2 tablespoons fish sauce

1 pound ground pork

2 teaspoons peanut oil

SAUCE

1 cup distilled white vinegar

⅓ cup packed light or dark brown sugar

2 garlic cloves, minced

2 small fresh red chiles, such as Thai bird, thinly sliced (seeds and ribs removed for less heat; see Tip, page 23)

2 tablespoons fresh lime juice (from 2 limes)

2 teaspoons fish sauce

Coconut Rice (page 84), for serving

Grated carrots, radishes, and lettuce, for serving

1 Make the meatballs: Using a mortar and pestle, smash the lemongrass, ginger, and garlic together to make a paste. Mince 2 whole scallions plus the white part of one more. Thinly slice the remaining green part and set it aside for garnish.

2 In a large bowl, toss together the lemongrass paste, minced scallions, cornstarch, and brown sugar. Add the fish sauce and the pork. Use your hands to gently combine the mixture without mixing it too much.

3 Form the pork mixture into about twenty 1-inch balls and set them on a plate. Refrigerate for at least 15 minutes.

4 Meanwhile, make the sauce: In a small saucepan, heat the vinegar and brown sugar, stirring occasionally, until the sugar has dissolved. Stir in the garlic. Let the mixture simmer until reduced by about half, 8 to 10 minutes. Add the chiles, lime juice, and fish sauce and remove from the heat. Let the sauce cool to room temperature.

5 Heat 1 teaspoon of the peanut oil in a 10-inch nonstick skillet over medium-high heat. Add half of the meatballs and cook, turning them often, until they are no longer pink in the center, 4 to 6 minutes. Transfer to a platter. Wipe the skillet out and repeat with the remaining oil and meatballs.

6 Sprinkle the meatballs with the scallion greens. Serve with coconut rice, carrots, radishes, lettuce, and the sauce.

Homemade fried rice really hits the spot. It takes very little effort, uses up forgotten leftover rice from the fridge, and is deeply satisfying when doused with hot sauce and eaten with a spoon. For this recipe, I use short-grain brown rice instead of white because I like its pleasant nuttiness, an excellent partner to the peanut oil and chopped nuts.

shrimp fried brown rice

SERVES 4 TO 6

¼ cup plus 1 teaspoon peanut oil

3 large eggs, lightly beaten

Kosher salt

⅓ cup minced peeled fresh ginger

5 garlic cloves, minced

6 scallions, trimmed and thinly sliced

1 cup shelled edamame, thawed if frozen

3 cups day-old cooked short-grain brown rice

8 ounces medium shrimp, peeled and deveined, halved lengthwise

¼ cup chopped roasted salted peanuts or cashews

Toasted sesame oil, for serving

1 In a large nonstick skillet or wok, heat the 1 teaspoon peanut oil over medium heat. Add the eggs and season with salt to taste. Cook, stirring occasionally, until the eggs are set but not too dry, 2 to 3 minutes. Use a spatula to tip the eggs out into a bowl.

2 Add the remaining ¼ cup peanut oil to the skillet and heat over medium-high heat. Add the ginger, garlic, and scallions and cook, stirring, until fragrant, 2 to 3 minutes. Add the edamame and cook until warmed through, about 3 minutes.

3 Add the rice and cook, stirring occasionally, until it is warmed through and crisp in spots, 6 to 8 minutes. Add the shrimp and cook, stirring, until just opaque throughout, about 3 minutes. Stir in the cooked eggs, then season to taste with salt. Top with the peanuts and a very light drizzle of sesame oil to serve.

---

tip Fried rice is best when made with leftover rice, but don't worry if you don't have any. Simply cook the rice according to the package directions, and then spread it out on a rimmed baking sheet to dry out for a few hours before proceeding with the recipe.

Consider this pizza crust the canvas for your new dinner masterpiece. You can paint it with anything you like. I've never been one for a saucy pie, which is why I decided to top this version with blistered cherry tomatoes and plenty of soft white cheese. For those who like the classics, try pepperoni, tomato sauce, and mozzarella.

white pizza with blistered tomatoes

SERVES 4

DOUGH

½ cup (90 g) potato starch

6 tablespoons (45 g) tapioca starch

½ cup (70 g) white rice flour

¼ cup millet flour

¼ cup milk powder

2 tablespoons psyllium husk powder

2 teaspoons sugar

1 teaspoon kosher salt

1¼ teaspoons instant yeast

¾ teaspoon baking powder

⅔ cup warm water (105° to 110°F)

1 large egg white, at room temperature

2 tablespoons neutral oil, such as safflower, plus more for the pan and brushing

1 In the bowl of a stand mixer, whisk together the potato starch, tapioca starch, white rice flour, millet flour, milk powder, psyllium husk powder, sugar, salt, yeast, and baking powder.

2 With the mixer running, pour in the water, egg white, and oil. Increase the speed to medium and beat the mixture until it is smooth and elastic, scraping down the sides of the bowl occasionally, about 3 minutes. The dough will look more like cookie dough than traditional pizza dough.

3 Scrape down the sides of the bowl and scoop the dough onto a lightly oiled piece of parchment. Using damp fingers, spread the dough out into a 10- to 11-inch round. Form a crust by making the edges a little thicker than the rest. Brush oil all over the surface.

4 Transfer the dough, still on the parchment, to a baking sheet and cover it with plastic wrap. Set it in a warm spot to rise for 1 hour. The dough won't double, but it will look a little puffier.

(RECIPE CONTINUES)

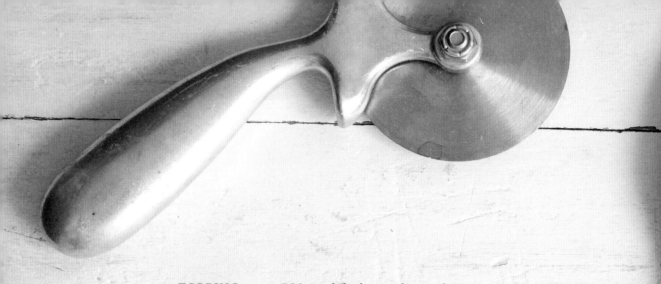

TOPPING

4 ounces fresh mozzarella cheese, cut into very thin slices (see Tip)

½ cup whole-milk ricotta cheese, homemade (page 28) or store-bought

¼ cup fresh basil leaves, chopped

2 tablespoons olive oil

12 ounces cherry tomatoes

Kosher salt

Aleppo or red pepper flakes, for sprinkling

5 Meanwhile, line a plate with paper towels, and lay the slices of mozzarella on the prepared plate. Top them with more paper towels and another plate. Let the mozzarella stand for at least 30 minutes to remove any excess water.

6 Preheat the oven to 425°F. Bake the dough until it is golden, puffed, and cooked through, 25 to 28 minutes.

7 While the pizza is baking, stir the ricotta and basil together in a bowl. In a large skillet, heat the oil over medium-high heat. Add the tomatoes and season with salt to taste. Cook the tomatoes until some have split and some are browned in spots, 8 to 10 minutes. Keep warm.

8 Top the baked pizza crust with the mozzarella, leaving a 1-inch border. Bake until the cheese has melted, about 2 minutes.

9 Remove the crust from the oven and top it with the tomatoes, dollops of the ricotta mixture, and a sprinkle of pepper flakes. Serve hot.

tips Some fresh mozzarellas are very moist; others are drier. To prevent soggy pizza, I like to press the cheese between paper towels before putting it on the pizza. If you'd like to skip this step, use part-skim mozzarella.

Be sure to let your flours come to room temperature if you stored them in the freezer.

I eat to live and I eat to enjoy. Sometimes that means broccoli and sometimes that means cake. Both ends of the spectrum are important. But I do believe in trying to add more value when you can. A delicious, decadent dish that has something good in it is a win-win, right? That's how this recipe evolved. I wanted a creamy dish reminiscent of both macaroni and cheese and risotto that would keep me full for longer. Chewy and lovely short-grain brown rice was the delicious solution.

cheesy skillet rice with bacon and peas

SERVES 4

2 slices bacon

3 tablespoons unsalted butter

1 small onion, finely chopped

1 small garlic clove, minced

1¼ cups short-grain brown rice

2½ cups chicken broth (page 20)

1 cup gluten-free breadcrumbs (see Tip)

¼ cup grated Parmigiano-Reggiano cheese

1 tablespoon arrowroot starch

1 cup whole milk

1 teaspoon gluten-free Dijon mustard

¾ cup grated Fontina cheese

¾ cup grated sharp cheddar cheese

1 cup frozen peas

1 teaspoon chopped fresh tarragon leaves

Kosher salt and freshly ground black pepper

1 In a 10-inch broiler-safe skillet, cook the bacon over medium heat until crisp, 6 to 8 minutes. Use a slotted spoon to transfer the bacon to a cutting board; then chop it and transfer it to a bowl. Add the butter to the bacon fat in the skillet and let it melt. Pour 2 tablespoons of this mixture into a small bowl and set it aside. Add the onions and garlic to the remaining fat in the skillet and cook, stirring occasionally, until softened and golden brown, about 8 minutes.

2 Add the rice to the skillet and cook it for a few minutes to toast it. Add the broth, bring the mixture to a boil, and then reduce the heat to a simmer. Cover the skillet and cook until most of the liquid has been absorbed and the rice is tender, 30 to 40 minutes.

3 Meanwhile, add the breadcrumbs and the Parmigiano to the reserved 2 tablespoons fat, and toss to mix. Preheat the broiler with a rack 8 inches below the heat source.

4 Sprinkle the arrowroot starch evenly over the cooked rice and stir to combine. Add the milk and bring the mixture to a simmer, stirring until it has thickened slightly, about 2 minutes. Stir in the bacon and the mustard, and then fold in the Fontina and the cheddar. Stir until the cheeses have melted. Stir in the peas and the tarragon, and season to taste with salt and pepper.

5 Remove the skillet from the heat and sprinkle the breadcrumb mixture evenly over the top. Broil just until the crumbs are golden brown and crisp, 30 seconds to 2 minutes. Be sure to carefully rotate the pan as necessary for even browning and keep an eye on it all times (broilers can be hot!). Let cool slightly before serving.

---

tip To make a crunchy topping I use fresh gluten-free breadcrumbs from day-old slices of the Simple Loaf of Bread on page 35. You could also use some of the leftover crispy brown rice cereal after making the Crispy Chocolate–Peanut Butter Bars on page 182.

This is my version of the classic Vietnamese *bun bo xao*. It has everything I want in a "pasta" salad: sweet, salty, and sour plus plenty of crunch. And it wholly satisfies all my noodle cravings. Save this recipe for dinner on a hot summer night—you never have to turn on the oven! If you'd like a little less spice, remove the ribs and seeds of the jalapeño before adding it in. On the other hand, a pleasantly tingling tongue is the perfect excuse for a post-dinner ice cream cone, if you ask me.

cold chicken and rice noodle salad

SERVES 4

12 ounces rice noodles

¼ cup fresh lime juice (from 2 to 3 limes)

3 tablespoons fish sauce

2 tablespoons peanut oil

1 to 2 fresh chiles, such as jalapeño or Thai bird chiles, sliced (see Tip, page 23)

2 garlic cloves, mashed with the side of a knife or using a mortar and pestle

2 teaspoons dark brown sugar

2 small carrots, peeled and cut into thin matchsticks

2 small Persian cucumbers, peeled and cut into matchsticks

1 cup cherry tomatoes, halved

1 cup mixed fresh tender herbs, such as cilantro, basil, and mint leaves, coarsely chopped, plus more for serving

1 cup shredded cooked chicken

1 ripe nectarine, pitted and thinly sliced

½ cup chopped roasted salted cashews or peanuts

1 Soak the rice noodles according to the package instructions and set aside.

2 In a large bowl, whisk together the lime juice, fish sauce, peanut oil, jalapeño, garlic, and brown sugar. Add the noodles, carrots, cucumbers, tomatoes, and herbs.

3 Serve the salad topped with the chicken, nectarine, nuts, and a sprinkle of extra herbs.

I have way too many kitchen gadgets; shopping for them is a weakness of mine. I was always in awe of my brother, who could whip up a delicious meal using only a 6-inch cutting board, a knife, and one pot. That said, sometimes the right tool makes all the difference. A potato ricer, which I use to make gnocchi, keeps the potatoes light and fluffy as it smashes them. If you don't have one, use a box grater to achieve a similar effect with a bit more effort.

sautéed lemony gnocchi

SERVES 4

2 medium russet potatoes (12 to 13 ounces each)

1 large egg

1 large egg yolk

Kosher salt

½ cup (80 g) sweet rice flour (see Tip)

¼ cup potato starch

2 tablespoons grated Parmigiano-Reggiano cheese, plus more for serving

4 tablespoons (½ stick) unsalted butter

1 teaspoon finely grated lemon zest

2 to 3 tablespoons fresh lemon juice

¼ cup mixed chopped fresh tender herbs, such as parsley or basil leaves

---

tip Sweet rice flour is made from glutinous or sticky rice. Look for it in Asian grocery stores and online.

1 Preheat the oven to 400°F. Set the potatoes on a roasting pan and pierce them all over with a fork. Bake the potatoes, rotating them occasionally, until they are very tender, about 1 hour. Remove them from the oven and let cool slightly.

2 When the potatoes are still warm but cool enough to handle, cut them in half and scoop out the flesh. Press the potato flesh through a potato ricer into a large bowl. You should have 12 ounces of potatoes. Set aside any extra potato flesh for another use.

3 While the potato flesh is still warm, add the egg, egg yolk, and 1½ teaspoons salt, and stir with a fork to combine. Add the sweet rice flour, potato starch, and cheese and stir to combine. Once a shaggy dough forms, knead the dough by hand in the bowl just until it comes together.

4 Tip the dough onto a piece of plastic wrap and form it into a disk. Cut the disk into 8 equal triangles. Take out one piece to work with and wrap the remaining dough and set it aside.

(RECIPE CONTINUES)

5 Using your hands, roll the dough to form a long rope about ¾ inch wide. Cut the rope into ¾-inch-long pieces. Transfer the pieces to a parchment-lined baking sheet and cover it with plastic wrap. Repeat with the remaining dough.

6 Bring a large pot of salted water to a boil. Add about a quarter of the gnocchi to the boiling water and cook until they float, 2 to 4 minutes. (Don't let them boil too vigorously or they may fall apart.) Use a slotted spoon to transfer them to another rimmed baking sheet. Repeat with the remaining gnocchi.

7 To finish, heat the butter in a 12-inch nonstick skillet over medium-high heat. Add the gnocchi and cook until they are golden brown in spots, shaking the pan occasionally to turn them over, 3 to 5 minutes. Add the lemon zest and juice, and swirl the skillet to combine. Toss in the herbs to coat. Serve hot, topped with extra cheese.

Crêpes make a pretty and sophisticated dinner. Here you have a simple roasted vegetable filling with cheesy scrambled eggs, but you could stuff the crêpes with whatever you have on hand. A little smoked ham and shredded Gruyère would be classic and tasty, or maybe some steamed asparagus and fried egg. For a breakfast treat, I like to fill them with bananas that I've sautéed with a little brown sugar, butter, and lime juice.

vegetable and egg–stuffed crêpes

SERVES 4

FILLING

1 pound shiitake mushrooms, stemmed and thinly sliced

8 ounces Lacinato kale, stemmed and thinly sliced

4 tablespoons olive oil

Kosher salt and freshly ground black pepper

1 teaspoon gluten-free Dijon mustard

2 tablespoons fresh lemon juice

6 large eggs, lightly beaten

3 ounces shredded Gruyère cheese (about ¾ cup)

1 cup fresh parsley leaves

BATTER

½ cup (70 g) brown rice flour

½ cup (70 g) millet flour

½ teaspoon kosher salt

1½ cups whole milk

2 large eggs

1 tablespoon olive oil, plus more for the pan

1 Make the filling: Preheat the oven to 425°F. In a bowl, toss the shiitakes and kale with 2 tablespoons of the olive oil, and season with salt and pepper to taste. Spread the vegetables out on a rimmed baking sheet and roast until tender and browned in spots, about 20 minutes, tossing them halfway through.

2 Meanwhile, make the dressing: In a small bowl, whisk the remaining 2 tablespoons olive oil with the Dijon mustard and lemon juice. Season the dressing with salt and pepper, and set it aside.

3 Prepare the batter: In a large bowl, whisk together the brown rice flour, millet flour, and salt. While whisking, slowly add the milk in a stream. Whisk in the eggs and the tablespoon of olive oil.

(RECIPE CONTINUES)

4 Heat about ½ teaspoon oil in a 10-inch nonstick skillet over medium heat. When the pan is hot, add a scant ¼ cup crêpe batter to one side of the pan and quickly tilt and swirl the pan to spread the batter to an even thickness. Cook until light golden and set on one side, about 1 minute. Tuck a small offset spatula under the edge of the crêpe, grab the crêpe with your fingers, and quickly flip it over. It will be hot, but if you work fast, you won't burn your fingers. Cook until light golden brown on the other side, 30 seconds to 1 minute. Slip the crêpe onto a baking sheet.

5 Continue with the rest of the batter and more oil as needed. The batter should make about 12 crêpes. Wipe out the skillet.

6 Make the filling: Add another ½ teaspoon oil to the skillet, and cook the eggs and cheese over medium-low heat until cooked to your liking. Season to taste with salt and pepper.

7 When the vegetables are tender, toss them in a large bowl with the parsley leaves and some of the dressing to taste. Fill each crêpe with vegetables and eggs, and serve.

Known as *socca* in France and *farinata* in Italy, this chickpea pancake is outstanding in any language. I make it with just chickpea flour, water, olive oil, and salt, but you can jazz it up with a few spices or herbs if you like. I find the pure flavor of this crispy, salty chickpea pancake addictive. It's excellent topped with a few vegetables and some cheese, too. If your *socca* sticks to the pan, give it a moment to cool down and then remove it one slice at a time.

SERVES 2 TO 4

¾ cup (90 g) chickpea flour

5 tablespoons extra virgin olive oil

1 teaspoon kosher salt, plus more to taste

1 medium shallot, thinly sliced

2 small red or orange bell peppers (6 ounces each), seeded and thinly sliced

2 tablespoons capers, rinsed and drained

Pinch of red pepper flakes

3 ounces good-quality smoked or fresh mozzarella cheese, thinly sliced

Fresh basil leaves, torn, for serving

italian-style chickpea socca

1 In a medium bowl, whisk together the chickpea flour, 2 tablespoons of the oil, the salt, and 1 cup of water until smooth. Set aside for 30 minutes.

2 Turn the oven to broil with a rack placed 6 inches below the heat source. In a well-seasoned 10-inch cast-iron skillet, heat 1 tablespoon of the oil over medium heat. Add the shallots and cook until translucent, 4 minutes. Add the bell peppers and cook until they are softened and browned in spots, about 8 minutes. Add the capers and red pepper flakes, and season to taste with salt. Transfer this mixture to a plate and keep it warm. Be sure to scrape out everything so nothing burns in the next step.

3 Set the skillet under the broiler to preheat for 5 to 10 minutes. Once the skillet is very hot, carefully remove it from the broiler, add the remaining 2 tablespoons oil, and swirl it to coat. Add the chickpea batter and return the skillet to the broiler. Broil until the *socca* is set, the edges are pulling away from the pan, and the top is crisp and browned in spots, about 8 minutes. Carefully remove the skillet from the oven and reduce the heat to 450°F.

4 Top the *socca* with the mozzarella and the bell pepper mixture, and return it to the oven. Cook until the cheese has melted, about 5 minutes. Let cool slightly before topping it with fresh basil. Serve hot.

This dish is impressive to behold and, even better, easy to make. I learned the method of cooking fish *en papillote* (in parchment) in my first month of culinary school. It is practically impossible to screw up, tastes great, and looks fancy—a real confidence booster.

I use this *en papillote* method for quick, light dinners whenever I can get my hands on fresh fish. Here I fill the packets with summery vegetables and whole slices of bright fresh lemon. Let your dinner companions open their own packets at the table. It's like opening a mouthwatering, fragrant present.

sole with vegetables en papillote

SERVES 4

1 lemon

1 medium zucchini, trimmed and thinly sliced

1 medium summer squash, trimmed and thinly sliced

Kosher salt and freshly ground black pepper

1 cup fresh basil leaves, torn

4 sole fillets (6 ounces each)

1 cup cherry tomatoes, halved

1 cup fresh corn kernels (from 2 ears)

4 teaspoons unsalted butter

2 to 3 tablespoons pine nuts, toasted

1 Preheat the oven to 450°F. Cut off the ends of the lemon, then cut off all the rind. Slice the lemon into thin rounds.

2 Start by making two of the four packets. Set two 12 × 16-inch rectangles of parchment on a work surface with a long side facing you. Crease each piece in half crosswise. Unfold the parchment and set one fourth of the zucchini and one fourth of the squash on the right side of each piece of paper. Season the vegetables with salt and pepper. Top each one with ¼ cup of the basil and 1 sole fillet. Then top each one with one fourth of the lemon slices, cherry tomatoes, and corn, plus 1 teaspoon of the butter; season with salt and pepper.

3 Fold the other half of the paper over the fish. To seal each packet, crimp the edges in a series of tight, overlapping folds all the way around. Repeat to make two more packets with the remaining fish, vegetables, butter, and seasoning.

4 Set the packets on two rimmed baking sheets and bake until the parchment has puffed and the fish is cooked through, 12 to 15 minutes. Transfer the packets to plates. Serve with the pine nuts.

I was lucky enough to enjoy my first taste of Spanish tortilla on a trip to Spain, and I was smitten from the first bite. Who could resist soft potatoes smothered in rich olive oil and salty eggs? I practically needed a tortilla fix every time we left the hotel. I even bought a big tortilla sandwich displayed in the murky glass box of a dubious food cart at the Barcelona train station. My brother thought I had lost my mind, but I'd still argue that the train station tortilla was the most delicious one I ate in all of Spain.

Making tortilla at home is simple—just don't fear the olive oil. You need a lot to make the potatoes properly silky. Most of it gets poured out before the eggs go in. But there's no need to let that flavored oil go to waste: serve the tortilla on slices of fresh ripe tomatoes and drizzle the whole thing with a bit of the leftover oil.

spanish tortilla

SERVES 4

¾ cup extra virgin olive oil

2 medium garlic cloves, thinly sliced

4 small Yukon Gold potatoes (about 1¼ pounds total), peeled, halved, and thinly sliced

½ small yellow onion, thinly sliced

Kosher salt

8 large eggs

1 teaspoon smoked paprika

½ cup packed fresh parsley leaves, chopped

1 In a 10-inch broiler-safe skillet, heat the oil and garlic over medium heat until the oil is hot. Add the potatoes, onions, and 2 teaspoons salt and cook, maintaining a gentle simmer, until the potatoes are tender but not browned, 10 to 15 minutes, gently flipping and stirring them to ensure even cooking.

2 Heat the broiler to high with a rack about 6 inches below the heat source. Meanwhile, in a large bowl, whisk together the eggs, paprika, and parsley. Using a slotted spoon, transfer the potatoes to the eggs. Without breaking up the potato slices, gently toss the egg mixture to evenly coat them. Pour the oil from the skillet into a small bowl, leaving about 1 teaspoon behind.

3 Pour the egg mixture back into the hot skillet and spread it out to an even thickness. Cook, without stirring, over medium heat until the eggs are mostly set with some loose egg in the center, 3 to 5 minutes. Transfer the skillet to the broiler and cook until the center is set, 1 to 2 minutes.

4 Let the tortilla stand at room temperature for a few minutes. Then use a rubber spatula to loosen the edges from the pan, cut into big wedges, and serve drizzled with some of the reserved oil.

I was certainly Italian in my last life. I have a love of pasta that runs deep. But the truth is, I'm not that great at making traditional wheat pasta from scratch. I can never get it quite thin enough. Homemade gluten-free pasta is my savior! Since there isn't any gluten, the dough doesn't fight back, and it is a cinch to roll out by hand—no pasta machine necessary. These ravioli have a lovely pea filling with a delicate sweet, creamy flavor, so I've paired them with a simple browned butter sauce. But you should feel free to use whatever sauce you like.

sweet pea and ricotta ravioli

**SERVES 4 TO 6
(MAKES ABOUT 30 RAVIOLI)**

FILLING

5 ounces frozen peas (about 1 cup)

½ cup whole-milk ricotta cheese, homemade (page 28) or store-bought

⅓ cup grated Pecorino Romano cheese (about ½ ounce), plus more for serving

1 teaspoon finely grated lemon zest

Kosher salt

DOUGH

½ cup (60 g) tapioca starch, plus more for dusting

¾ cup (115 g) sweet rice flour (see Tip, page 131)

¾ cup (90 g) chickpea flour

4 teaspoons psyllium husk powder

1½ teaspoons kosher salt

2 large eggs

2 tablespoons extra virgin olive oil

1 Make the filling: Bring a small pot of salted water to a boil. Add the peas and cook just until warmed through, about 1 minute. Drain the peas, transfer them to the bowl of a food processor, and blend until almost smooth. Transfer the puree to a bowl and stir in the ricotta, Pecorino, lemon zest, and salt to taste. Cover and refrigerate until ready to use.

2 Make the dough: Lightly dust a baking sheet with tapioca starch and set it aside. In a large bowl, whisk together the sweet rice flour, chickpea flour, tapioca starch, psyllium husk powder, and salt. In a small bowl, whisk together the eggs, olive oil, and ¼ cup of water. Add the egg mixture to the flour mixture and stir until the flours are evenly moistened.

3 Lightly dust a work surface with tapioca starch. Knead the dough with your hands in the bowl until it starts to come together; then tip the dough out onto the work surface and knead it until it is smooth. It will come together in a ball but the dough will be a bit sticky. Cut the dough into 8 pieces to make it easier to work with. Reserve one piece and wrap the remaining pieces in plastic wrap.

(RECIPE CONTINUES)

tip I've found that a mini pin offers more control for pasta (and dumplings!). Mine came from the hardware store. Just ask the clerk to trim a ¾-inch dowel to a length of 10 inches.

SAUCE

6 tablespoons unsalted butter

3 garlic cloves, thinly sliced

Pinch of red pepper flakes

Pinch of kosher salt

4 Make the ravioli: Dust a work surface and a rolling pin with tapioca starch. Roll the piece of dough to form an even rectangle, as thin as you can make it without any cracks or rips. It should be about a scant ⅛ inch thick and you should be able to see through it. Repeat the same process with another piece of dough.

5 Use a 2¼-inch round cookie cutter to cut out the rolled dough. Brush the edges of half of the rounds lightly with water, and then dollop a heaping teaspoon of the pea filling onto the center. Carefully lay the other rounds of dough on top of the filling. Gently press the air out from around the filling, and then crimp the edges with a fork. Transfer the ravioli to the prepared baking sheet. Repeat the process with the remaining dough, rerolling the scraps as necessary to use up the filling. You should have about 30 ravioli.

6 Make the sauce: Melt the butter in a large skillet over medium heat and cook, swirling the butter occasionally, until the foam subsides and the milk solids at the bottom of the pan turn golden brown. Add the garlic, red pepper flakes, and salt, and cook over medium-low heat, stirring occasionally, until the garlic is golden and soft, 30 seconds to 1 minute. Keep warm.

7 Cook the ravioli: Bring a large pot of salted water to a boil. Add 8 to 10 ravioli to the boiling water and cook, stirring very gently so they don't stick to the bottom, until the dough is cooked through and the ravioli have been floating for at least 30 seconds, about 3 minutes. Use a slotted spoon to transfer the ravioli to a platter or serving bowls. Repeat with the remaining ravioli.

8 To serve, drizzle the ravioli with the browned butter sauce, and toss gently to coat. Serve with extra Pecorino Romano.

Day-old quinoa can be a sad thing. Freshly made quinoa is fluffy and nutty, delicious topped with practically anything. On the second day, after a night languishing in the fridge, it deflates like a helium balloon well after the party is over. I mean to eat it so it won't go to waste, but I rarely do.

That's where these cute little cakes come in. When dry leftover quinoa snuggles up to roasted sweet potato and plenty of smoky chipotle and sharp cheddar, it is reborn into something wonderful. I like these flavorful patties over a bowl of greens and topped with a fried egg (and maybe even a little more cheese and some sliced avocado).

chipotle-spiced quinoa cakes

SERVES 4

2 tablespoons unsalted butter, plus more for the skillet

1 small onion, chopped

3 garlic cloves, minced

2 tablespoons chopped chipotle in adobo (less if you'd like less heat)

1¾ cups cooked quinoa

½ cup (50 g) oat flour

1 cup mashed baked sweet potato (from 1 small sweet potato)

2 teaspoons finely grated lime zest (from 1 lime)

4 ounces (about 1 cup) sharp cheddar cheese, grated, plus more for serving

Kosher salt

1 large egg

Lime wedges, for serving

1 avocado, peeled, pitted, and sliced, for serving (optional)

1 In a 10-inch nonstick skillet, heat the 2 tablespoons butter over medium heat. Add the onions, garlic, and chipotle and cook until the onions are translucent, about 8 minutes. Let cool slightly.

2 In a medium bowl, combine the quinoa, oat flour, sweet potato, lime zest, cheese, and the onion mixture. Season to taste with salt. Stir in the egg. With your hands, divide the mixture into 8 small patties, about ¼ cup each.

3 Heat some butter in a 10-inch nonstick skillet over medium-high heat. Cook 4 of the patties at a time until crisp and golden on the outside and warm all the way through, flipping them halfway through, about 6 minutes total. Transfer the cooked patties to a plate and keep warm. Repeat with the remaining patties. Serve with lime wedges, extra cheese, and avocado if desired.

sweet and savory snacks

A little bite between meals is one of life's great pleasures. And snacking usually complements other joyful activities. A good book and a snack. A movie and a snack. A cocktail and a snack. A good friend, a chat, and a snack. All experiences are more fun with the addition of a delicious nibble.

I know that the simplicity of premade gluten-free snacks is tempting. But all those processed foods aren't worth it. Homemade gluten-free snacks are not only delicious but also fun to customize. Once you make the Loaded Oat Bars (page 161) or the Peach-Raspberry Swirl Fruit Leather (page 166), for example, I know you'll want to experiment with other nuts and fruits. Try making the Parmesan Cheese Crackers (page 156) with cheddar, or switch out the rosemary in the Rosemary Amaranth Crisps (page 153) for another of your favorite herbs. The possibilities are endless when you look past the snack aisle and cook at home instead.

I never developed any skill at the piano. Despite my failings, I persisted for eight ear-shattering years of lessons. Truth be told, I was in it for the snacks—both of my piano teachers rewarded my terrible playing with treats. Those lessons instilled more than an appreciation of music: a lifelong love of chocolate and toffee popcorn.

chocolate toffee popcorn

MAKES 8 TO 10 CUPS

4 teaspoons vegetable oil

6 tablespoons popcorn kernels

1 cup coarsely chopped pecans

8 tablespoons (1 stick) unsalted butter, plus more for the pans

1 cup sugar

1 teaspoon kosher salt, plus more for sprinkling

½ teaspoon pure vanilla extract

½ teaspoon baking soda

12 ounces bittersweet chocolate, finely chopped

1 In a large pot, heat the oil over medium-high heat. When it is hot, add the popcorn kernels and cover the pot. Once the popcorn starts to pop, reduce the heat to medium. Hold the lid on the pot and shake the pot until the popping stops. Transfer the popped popcorn to a large bowl and discard any unpopped kernels. Add the pecans.

2 Butter two large rimmed baking sheets. In a medium-sized heavy-bottomed pot with a candy thermometer attached, heat the butter, sugar, salt, and 2 tablespoons water over medium heat, swirling the pot occasionally, until the butter has melted. Cook the mixture until the candy thermometer reads 300°F. Then remove the pot from the heat and quickly stir in the vanilla. Be careful; it will spatter a bit. Stir in the baking soda.

3 Carefully pour the mixture over the popcorn, and immediately stir the popcorn well to coat it in the warm toffee. Spread the coated popcorn out on the prepared baking sheets, and sprinkle with salt. Let the popcorn stand until it is completely cool.

4 Transfer the chocolate to a double boiler or large heat proof bowl set over a pot of barely simmering water. Melt the chocolate, stirring it occasionally. Line a rimmed baking sheet with parchment.

5 Carefully drop a few pieces of popcorn into the melted chocolate and flip it around with two forks. Lift the coated popcorn out, tap it against the side of the bowl to remove any excess chocolate, and transfer it to the parchment-lined baking sheet. Repeat with half of the remaining popcorn. Transfer the chocolate-dipped popcorn to the fridge until set, about 20 minutes. Extra chocolate can be cooled, wrapped in plastic, and used again.

6 When the chocolate popcorn has set, toss it with the plain toffee popcorn in a large bowl, and serve. Store in an airtight container in the fridge for up to 2 days.

Smoked paprika is made from pimiento peppers that are dried, smoked over an oak fire, and ground. It's mild and sweet and delicious. Here I've paired it with plenty of garlic and a little fresh thyme for a flavorful popcorn topper. Sneak it into the movies—if your date thinks good popcorn is more important than a little garlic breath, you've got a keeper.

smoky garlic popcorn

MAKES 8 TO 10 CUPS

4 teaspoons vegetable oil

6 tablespoons popcorn kernels

3 tablespoons unsalted butter

2 garlic cloves, smashed to a paste

1 teaspoon smoked paprika

1 teaspoon chopped fresh thyme leaves

Kosher salt, for sprinkling

1 In a large pot, heat the oil over medium-high heat. When it is hot, add the popcorn kernels and cover the pot. Once the popcorn starts to pop, reduce the heat to medium. Hold the lid on the pot and shake the pot until the popping stops. Transfer the popped popcorn to a large bowl and discard any unpopped kernels.

2 In a small skillet, melt the butter over medium heat. Add the garlic, paprika, and thyme and cook, stirring, until the garlic is tender but not browned, about 5 minutes.

3 Little by little, drizzle the butter mixture over the popcorn and toss to coat the popcorn evenly. Sprinkle with kosher salt to taste.

Here I've dressed up cannellini beans with preserved lemon, shallots, and parsley—an extraordinarily tasty combination. The salty, briny lemons bring out the savory essence of the cannellinis, and a little sumac heightens the tang. It's lovely as a dip with crackers, but it can work in so many other ways. Try it as a warm puree under seared scallops or slathered on bread as part of your favorite turkey sandwich. Layered on toast with sprouts and avocado, it makes an excellent tartine.

white bean dip with preserved lemon

MAKES ABOUT 2 CUPS

2 tablespoons extra virgin olive oil, plus more for drizzling

¼ cup finely chopped shallots

2 cups cooked cannellini beans, with a few tablespoons cooking water reserved (see Tip)

¼ cup chopped preserved lemon, homemade (page 25) or store-bought

¼ cup packed fresh parsley leaves

Kosher salt

Ground sumac, for sprinkling (see Tip, page 22)

Aleppo or red pepper flakes, for sprinkling

1 In a 10-inch nonstick skillet, heat the oil over medium heat. Add the shallots and cook until golden and softened, 6 to 8 minutes.

2 In the bowl of a food processor, combine the beans, preserved lemon, and parsley and process until smooth. Add a tablespoon of the bean broth if necessary to achieve a nice creamy texture. Add the shallots, with their oil, to the bean mixture and process until smooth. Season to taste with salt if necessary (depending on how salty your lemon is, you may not need additional seasoning).

3 Transfer the dip to a serving bowl, drizzle with olive oil, and sprinkle with sumac and pepper flakes.

tip This recipe works well with both home-cooked beans (see page 30) and canned beans that have been rinsed and drained. Instead of cooking water, you can use a little tap water to thin out the puree if necessary.

white bean dip with
preserved lemon, page 151

Grassy amaranth flour and piney rosemary are really a perfect match and create a flavorful cracker when baked along with almond flour and really good fruity olive oil. These crisps are wonderful with soup, a little labneh (see page 26), your favorite cheese, or the White Bean Dip with Preserved Lemon (page 151).

rosemary amaranth crisps

MAKES 3 TO 4 DOZEN CRACKERS

2 cups (180 g) almond flour

2 cups (210 g) amaranth flour

2 teaspoons kosher salt, plus more for sprinkling

1 teaspoon baking powder

4 teaspoons chopped fresh rosemary leaves

1 large egg

¼ cup good-quality extra virgin olive oil

1 large egg white

1 Preheat the oven to 350°F. In the bowl of a food processor, combine the almond flour, amaranth flour, salt, baking powder, and rosemary and pulse to combine. Add the whole egg, olive oil, and ¼ cup of water, and blend until a dough forms. Add up to 1 more tablespoon of water if necessary. Tip the dough out onto a piece of parchment on a work surface, and form it into a disk.

2 Roll the dough out to a scant ⅛-inch thickness. The dough will be a bit crumbly and may break apart. If it does, simply push the dough back together. Use a fluted pastry wheel to cut the dough into roughly 2 × 2½-inch rectangles. If you like, you can trim the edges and reroll the scraps on another piece of parchment. Transfer the dough, still on the parchment, to a baking sheet and wrap well with plastic. Freeze until firm, 15 to 30 minutes.

3 In a small bowl, lightly beat the egg white. Brush half of the frozen crackers with egg white, and then sprinkle with salt. Use an offset spatula to lift and separate the seasoned crackers and transfer them to two parchment-lined baking sheets. Bake until the crackers are golden brown and set, rotating the sheets halfway through, 18 to 22 minutes.

4 Transfer the crackers, on the parchment sheets, to a rack to cool completely. Repeat with the remaining crackers. Store the cooled baked crackers in an airtight container in the freezer and bring to room temperature before serving.

Making tortilla chips from scratch certainly takes more effort than buying a bag at the supermarket, but it's worth it. When you start with a good-quality masa harina, the chips have a delightful corn flavor. Try these with your favorite tomato salsa or crumbled over a bowl of chili (see page 101).

(see page 101)

MAKES ABOUT 8 DOZEN

1¾ cups (210 g) gluten-free masa harina, plus more as needed

1 tablespoon finely grated lime zest (from 2 limes)

¼ teaspoon cayenne pepper, plus more to taste

1 tablespoon kosher salt

Neutral oil, such as safflower, for brushing, plus more for the pans

Lime wedges, for serving

spicy baked tortilla chips

1 In a large bowl, whisk together the masa harina, 1½ teaspoons of the lime zest, ⅛ teaspoon of the cayenne pepper, and ½ teaspoon of the salt. Add 1¼ cups hot water and stir the mixture until it comes together into a smooth ball. It should feel soft and clammy but not wet. If the dough is too sticky, it will stick to the parchment paper while you're working with it, so add a bit more masa harina. If the dough is too dry, add a bit more water. Wrap it in plastic wrap, and let it rest at room temperature for at least 30 minutes and up to 2 hours.

2 Preheat the oven to 400°F. In a small bowl, combine the remaining lime zest, ⅛ teaspoon cayenne pepper (or more to taste), and 2½ teaspoons salt; set aside. Cut out twenty-four 6-inch squares of parchment.

3 Cut the dough into 12 equal pieces and form each piece into a ball. Work with 1 ball of dough at a time and cover the rest with plastic. Set one of the squares of parchment on a work surface, place a dough ball on top, and cover it with another square of parchment. Use a flat plate to press the dough into a flat round. Then use a rolling pin to roll the dough into a very thin 6-inch round. It should be a scant ⅛ inch thick. Repeat this process with the rest of the dough.

4 Oil two large rimmed baking sheets. Remove the parchment and cut each dough round into 8 triangles. Transfer the triangles to the prepared baking sheets. Brush the triangles lightly with oil and sprinkle with the lime-salt mixture.

5 Bake until the chips are crispy and lightly browned around the edges, 15 to 20 minutes, rotating the sheets and tossing the chips halfway through. They will firm up a bit more as they cool. Spritz the chips with lime juice to serve. Store the chips in an airtight container at room temperature for up to 3 days.

---

tip If you would like to make fresh corn tortillas, stop after step 3 and simply cook the shaped dough rounds in a hot cast-iron skillet until puffed slightly and browned in spots, 1 to 2 minutes per side.

Go ahead and spend a few extra bucks on genuine Parmigiano-Reggiano. The imported stuff is really special, and since these crackers have so few ingredients, the quality of the cheese will make all the difference.

parmesan cheese crackers

MAKES ABOUT 6 CUPS OF CRACKERS

1 cup (140 g) brown rice flour (see Tip)

1 cup (145 g) sweet rice flour

1 teaspoon kosher salt, plus more for sprinkling

8 tablespoons (1 stick) unsalted butter, at room temperature

7½ ounces Parmigiano-Reggiano cheese, finely grated (about 3½ cups)

4 to 6 tablespoons ice water

1 large egg white, lightly beaten

---

tip I recommend using a finely milled brown rice flour, like Bob's Red Mill brand, for the best texture.

1 In the bowl of a food processor, combine the rice flours and the salt and pulse to combine. Add the butter and the Parmigiano and pulse until very well combined. Add 4 tablespoons of the ice water and pulse until the dough is just wet enough to come together when squeezed. Add up to 2 tablespoons more ice water if necessary.

2 Tip the dough onto a work surface and form it into a disk. Cut the disk in half. Wrap one half in plastic wrap and refrigerate it.

3 On a piece of parchment, roll the other piece of the dough out to a scant ⅛-inch thickness. Use a fluted pastry wheel to cut the dough into ¾-inch-wide strips. Then cut the strips in the other direction to make ¾-inch squares. Use the flat end of a wooden skewer to poke a hole in the center of each square. Transfer the dough squares, still on the parchment, to a baking sheet and freeze until firm, about 15 minutes. Repeat with the remaining dough. Preheat the oven to 350°F.

4 Brush one sheet of crackers with the egg white and sprinkle with salt. Use an offset spatula to gently break the seasoned crackers apart, and space them about 1 inch apart on a parchment-lined baking sheet. Bake until the crackers are puffed, set, and browned on the bottom, 15 to 18 minutes. (Make sure to cook them well so that the finished crackers are crisp.)

5 Transfer the baked crackers, still on the parchment, to a cooling rack. Repeat with the remaining frozen crackers. Store the cooled crackers in an airtight container at room temperature for up to 5 days or freeze them for up to a month.

The coconut-laden chickpea curry my grandmother used to make inspired this easy recipe. Salty, spicy, and sweet—it's everything you want in an addictive snack. If you don't plan on serving these guys right away, toast the coconut separately and then add it in just before serving so that it stays nice and crisp.

MAKES ABOUT 2½ CUPS

3½ cups cooked chickpeas (see Tip)

3 tablespoons melted coconut oil (see Tip, page 175)

4 teaspoons finely grated lime zest (from 1 lime)

1 small fresh chile, such as Thai bird or serrano, minced (ribs and seeds removed for less heat) (see Tip, page 23)

Kosher salt

1 cup unsweetened flaked coconut

Lime wedges, for serving

coconut roasted chickpeas

1 Preheat the oven to 400°F. Set the chickpeas on a paper-towel-lined rimmed baking sheet. Roll the chickpeas around on the towels to remove as much excess water as you can. You can remove the skins if you see some of them separating, but it's not essential.

2 Remove the paper towels and toss the chickpeas on the baking sheet with the coconut oil, lime zest, and chile, and season to taste with salt. Roast until the color of the chickpeas darkens and they are almost crisp, 20 to 30 minutes.

3 Carefully toss the coconut with the chickpeas, and return the baking sheet to the oven. Bake just until the coconut is golden brown, 4 to 6 minutes. (Keep an eye on it, as coconut can burn quickly.) Transfer the sheet to a rack to cool. Squeeze a few lime wedges over the chickpeas before serving.

tip This recipe works well with both home-cooked beans (see page 30) and canned beans that have been rinsed and drained.

Most people love serving deviled eggs at parties. But seeing a platter of them just stresses me out because I want the eggs all to myself. I get a bit uneasy when I see other people eating them. I worry, wondering how there is ever going to be enough. (And how can I eat twelve halves without anyone noticing?)

That's why I've started making them as a snack, at home—so I can get my fill. Four halves plus two cocktails add up to a perfect predinner treat for two. I add quickly pickled shallots for a treat reminiscent of mignonette sauce. Feel free to double the amount in step 1 and use the extra shallots in your next sandwich. Yum!

deviled eggs with pickled shallots

SERVES 4

1 small shallot, very thinly sliced

1 tablespoon sherry vinegar

Pinch of sugar

Kosher salt

4 large eggs

3 tablespoons Mayonnaise, homemade (page 27) or store-bought

1 teaspoon gluten-free Dijon mustard

¼ teaspoon smoked paprika, plus more for sprinkling

Fresh parsley leaves, for garnish

1 In a small bowl, toss the shallots with the vinegar, sugar, and ½ teaspoon salt. Set aside for at least 30 minutes or up to 8 hours.

2 Meanwhile, add the eggs to a pot of cold water and bring to a boil. Remove from the heat, cover the pot, and let the eggs stand for 15 minutes. Then drain and peel the eggs. Carefully slice them in half and pop the yolks into a medium bowl.

3 Mash the egg yolks with the mayonnaise, Dijon mustard, and smoked paprika. Drain the shallots, reserving the vinegar mixture, and mince enough shallots to equal 4 teaspoons. Stir the minced shallots and a splash of the vinegar mixture into the yolk mixture. Season to taste with salt. (Be careful with the salt. You may not need any.)

4 Spoon the yolk mixture into the egg whites. (If you'd like to be extra-fancy, transfer the filling to a pastry bag fitted with a star tip and pipe it into the egg whites.) Top each egg with some of the remaining pickled shallots, a few parsley leaves, and a sprinkling of paprika.

For this recipe I took the crunchy granola bar recipe from my first book and adapted it to make a soft oat bar with the addition of creamy almond butter. The results are tender and lovely—a perfect gluten-free treat for packing in lunch boxes and picnic baskets.

loaded oat bars

MAKES 1 DOZEN BARS

½ cup melted coconut oil, plus more for greasing the pan (see Tip, page 175)

1¾ cups old-fashioned rolled oats

¾ cup chopped pecans

½ cup chopped pitted dried Medjool dates (see Tip, page 196)

½ cup chopped dried cherries

¾ cup unsweetened shredded coconut

½ cup millet

¼ cup almond flour

1 teaspoon ground cinnamon

1 teaspoon kosher salt

⅓ cup packed dark brown sugar

⅓ cup Lyle's Golden Syrup or honey

½ cup unsweetened natural almond butter

1 Preheat the oven to 350°F. Grease a 9-inch square baking pan with coconut oil and line it with parchment, leaving a 2-inch overhang on two sides. In a large bowl, combine the oats, pecans, dates, cherries, coconut, millet, almond flour, cinnamon, and salt. Make sure to break up the dates—they tend to clump together.

2 Clip a candy thermometer to the side of a small saucepan, and heat the brown sugar, Lyle's Golden Syrup, and 2 tablespoons of water over medium-high heat. If the sugar mixture is too low in the pan, the temperature won't register properly on the thermometer. To fix this, hold the pan at an angle while it cooks so the tip of the thermometer stays in the syrup. Cook until the sugar reaches 248°F, 4 to 5 minutes; then remove the pan from the heat and whisk in the coconut oil and the almond butter.

3 Add the sugar mixture to the oat mixture and stir to combine. Transfer the mixture to the prepared baking pan and flatten it to an even thickness. Use a spatula or your hands to really push and compact the mixture.

4 Bake until the mixture is set and deep golden brown, 28 to 32 minutes. Let it cool completely in the pan on a rack. Then, using the parchment, transfer it to a cutting board and cut it into bars. Wrap each bar in plastic wrap or parchment. Store in an airtight container at room temperature for up to 5 days or in the freezer for up to a month.

tip If you want to go the extra mile, dip each bar in some melted chocolate.

I would guess that you don't need much convincing to try this one. The simple combination of chocolate, caramel, and nuts is a classic. A little salt and some cayenne make it sublime.

MAKES 2 DOZEN CLUSTERS

2½ cups walnut halves, toasted and cooled

1 cup sugar

¼ cup Lyle's Golden Syrup or honey

½ cup heavy cream

4 tablespoons (½ stick) unsalted butter, cut into pieces

½ teaspoon kosher salt

4 ounces bittersweet chocolate, melted and cooled slightly

Flaky sea salt, for sprinkling

Cayenne pepper, for sprinkling

caramel walnut clusters

1 Line a large rimmed baking sheet with a silicone baking mat or a lightly greased piece of parchment. Arrange the walnuts into 24 small piles.

2 In a medium-sized heavy saucepan, heat the sugar and ¼ cup of water over medium-high heat. Cook, occasionally gently swirling the pan (not stirring), until the sugar is a medium amber color, 6 to 9 minutes. Remove the pan from the heat and stir in the Lyle's Golden Syrup until dissolved.

3 Return the pan to the heat, clip on a candy thermometer, and stir in the heavy cream, butter, and kosher salt. Be careful; it will spatter and steam. Cook the mixture until it reaches 248°F. Remove the pan from the heat, and let the mixture cool until it is pourable but very thick, 5 to 10 minutes. Then spoon about a tablespoon of the caramel over each nut cluster. Let the clusters cool to room temperature.

4 Spoon a dollop of melted chocolate onto each cluster; then sprinkle with sea salt and cayenne. Let the clusters harden at room temperature before serving (or feel free to eat them gooey and warm). Store in an airtight container in the fridge for up to 1 week. Let them stand at room temperature to soften a bit before serving.

Traditionally graham crackers are made with graham flour, an unrefined mixture of wheat flour, wheat germ, and wheat bran. For my tasty gluten-free version I rely on neutral almond flour mixed with brown rice and oat flours for nuttiness. Molasses and brown sugar give these crackers their spicy sweetness. They're delicious smeared with peanut butter and served with milk. Or use them to make the crust for the cheesecake on page 176.

cinnamon graham crackers

MAKES ABOUT 20 CRACKERS

1½ cups (135 g) almond flour

½ cup (70 g) brown rice flour

½ cup (50 g) oat flour

½ cup packed light brown sugar

¼ cup tapioca starch, plus more for rolling

1 teaspoon baking powder

½ teaspoon baking soda

½ teaspoon kosher salt

1½ teaspoons ground cinnamon

8 tablespoons (1 stick) unsalted butter, at room temperature but not too soft, cut into pieces

¼ cup molasses

1 With an electric mixer on medium speed, combine the almond flour, brown rice flour, oat flour, brown sugar, tapioca starch, baking powder, baking soda, salt, and cinnamon until well mixed. Add the butter and molasses, and blend until well combined. Tip the dough out onto a work surface. You may have to knead it a few times to make sure all of the molasses is evenly distributed. Divide the dough in half and form two small rectangles, wrap them in plastic wrap, and refrigerate until cold, at least 1 hour and up to overnight.

2 Preheat the oven to 350°F. Place one dough rectangle on a sheet of parchment and cover it with another sheet of parchment. Roll the dough to form an 8¼ × 10¼-inch rectangle with a short side facing you. It should be about ⅛ inch thick. Trim ¼ inch off the edges. Cut the rectangle in half lengthwise, and then cut it crosswise into 2-inch-wide pieces to create 10 rectangles. Score each rectangle in half crosswise but don't cut all the way through. Using a fork, make three indentations in each square. Transfer the dough, still on the parchment, to a baking sheet and freeze it for 15 minutes. Repeat with the other rectangle.

3 Bake the first sheet of dough until the edges of the rectangles have darkened slightly and the crackers are set and dry, rotating the sheet halfway through, 15 to 18 minutes. While the crackers are still warm, use a knife to cut them apart, and reinforce the fork marks if desired. Repeat with the other sheet of dough. Let the crackers cool completely on the baking sheets on a rack.

I wanted to figure out a way to enjoy the classic Eastern flavors of cardamom and coffee past my morning cup. Enter almonds, the satisfying and healthful-anytime snack. Coating nuts in chocolate, coffee, and cardamom makes them irresistible. Thank goodness they're portable!

mocha cardamom almonds

MAKES 2 CUPS

Coconut oil, for greasing the pan

⅓ cup packed light brown sugar

2 tablespoons unsweetened Dutch-process cocoa powder

1 tablespoon ground coffee

½ teaspoon cardamom seeds

½ teaspoon kosher salt

2 cups raw almonds

1 tablespoon beaten egg white

1 Preheat the oven to 300°F. Grease a rimmed baking sheet with coconut oil. In a clean spice grinder or coffee mill, process the brown sugar, cocoa powder, coffee, cardamom seeds, and salt until a fine powder forms.

2 In a medium bowl, toss the almonds with the egg white until evenly moistened. Add the sugar mixture and toss gently to coat.

3 Transfer the nuts to the prepared rimmed baking sheet and spread them out in an even layer. Bake until the nuts smell fragrant and are dry, stirring them halfway through, 18 to 24 minutes. Let the nuts cool completely on the baking sheet on a rack. Store in an airtight container at room temperature for up to 1 week or in the freezer for up to 1 month.

Making fruit leather takes nothing but a bit of patience. I like to make this in the dead of winter, when a fresh peach hasn't grazed my lips in what feels like an eternity. Frozen fruit—which is less expensive and still delicious—is available anytime, and the warmth of an oven kept on low heat for hours is welcome and cozy.

peach-raspberry swirl fruit leather

MAKES ABOUT 1 DOZEN PIECES

12 ounces frozen raspberries

12 ounces frozen peaches

¼ cup sugar or honey

tip Convection baking is really the best way to make fruit leather, but if your oven doesn't have a convection setting, bake the leather at the same temperature. It will just take a bit longer.

1 In two medium saucepans, heat the raspberries and the peaches separately over medium-high heat, stirring occasionally, until the fruit has broken down and some of the liquid has evaporated, 15 to 20 minutes. Remove from the heat.

2 Carefully transfer the cooked raspberries to the bowl of a food processor, and blend until the mixture is smooth. Set a medium-mesh sieve over a bowl and pass the raspberry puree through, using a spoon to help the mixture along. Discard the seeds. You should have ½ cup of strained puree. Add 2 tablespoons of the sugar to the raspberry puree.

3 Rinse out the bowl of the food processor and blend the cooked peaches until smooth. Transfer the puree to a bowl. Stir in 2 tablespoons of the sugar. Preheat the oven to 200°F, on the convection setting if available.

4 Set a silicone baking mat into a large rimmed baking sheet. Spread the peach puree in an even layer, leaving a 1-inch border. Top the peach with dollops of the raspberry puree. Use an offset spatula to spread and swirl the purees to make one even layer. Bake until the surface is just tacky to the touch but not wet, 2 to 3 hours (on convection). Let the fruit leather dry at room temperature, 1 to 2 hours.

5 Peel the sheet of fruit leather off of the silicone mat and transfer it to a sheet of parchment. Roll the parchment up with the fruit leather. Cut the roll into slices and store them in an airtight container at room temperature for up to 2 weeks.

desserts

Making dessert is my number one passion, and treating a friend to a homemade dessert is how I show my love. But over the past few years, many of my friends and loved ones have given up gluten. Inspired by them, I've concentrated on figuring out new ways to make sweets without the wheat. Going gluten-free shouldn't mean going cake-free!

Thankfully making gluten-free desserts is surprisingly easy. More important, they can be decadent and wonderfully tasty. When you remove the wheat flour from your desserts, you make space for delicious and nutritious alternatives. A chewy hazelnut cookie or a tender cake made with almond flour will satisfy any sweet tooth. From simple afternoon snacks like Oatmeal–Chocolate Chunk Ice Cream Sandwiches (page 187) and Macaroon Brownies (page 179) to more party-worthy desserts like Blueberry Shortbread Pandowdy (page 170) and Raspberry Cream Tart with Pistachios (page 199), no one will ever miss the wheat.

I'm a sucker for historical reenactments. Old Sturbridge Village, the living museum that re-creates life in eighteenth-century rural New England, is one of my favorite places on Earth. I just love to get swept away in the past. My love of history occasionally spills into my dessert-making as well. A pandowdy is an old-fashioned American dessert, probably invented sometime in the 1800s. It's pie's dowdier cousin. It was traditionally made by topping fruit with leftover dough scraps. I like to bake the shortbread biscuits separately for a few minutes to crisp them up, then layer them on the fruit filling. This ensures the perfect combination of a crunchy top and a fruit-soaked bottom.

blueberry shortbread pandowdy

SERVES 6 TO 8

DOUGH

½ cup (45 g) almond flour

½ cup (50 g) oat flour

⅓ cup sugar

¼ cup brown rice flour

6 tablespoons (45 g) tapioca starch, plus more for rolling

1 tablespoon psyllium husk powder

¾ teaspoon kosher salt

8 tablespoons (1 stick) cold unsalted butter, cut into pieces

1 large egg, lightly beaten

FILLING

6 cups fresh or frozen wild blueberries (thawed if frozen)

2 tablespoons cornstarch

⅓ cup sugar

½ teaspoon freshly grated lemon zest

½ teaspoon freshly ground cardamom

1 tablespoon unsalted butter, cut into pieces

1 large egg white, lightly beaten

¼ cup sliced almonds

1 Make the dough: In the bowl of a food processor, combine the almond flour, oat flour, sugar, brown rice flour, tapioca starch, psyllium husk powder, and salt and pulse to combine. Add the butter and pulse until the mixture resembles coarse meal. Add the whole egg and pulse until the dough comes together.

2 Lightly dust a piece of parchment with tapioca starch. Tip the dough out onto the prepared parchment, dust it lightly with tapioca starch, and roll it into a 10 × 9-inch rectangle. Cut the dough into 16 equal pieces. Transfer the dough, still on the parchment, to a baking sheet and freeze it for 20 minutes. Preheat the oven to 350°F with racks in the middle and lower third of the oven.

3 Meanwhile, make the filling: Combine the blueberries, cornstarch, sugar, lemon zest, and cardamom in a 2-quart baking dish. Top evenly with the butter pieces.

(RECIPE CONTINUES)

4 Brush the top of the dough pieces with the egg white and top with the almonds. Use an offset spatula to separate the frozen pieces. Bake the dough pieces on the middle oven rack and the fruit on the bottom rack for 25 minutes.

5 Stir the fruit and top it with the shortbread pieces, overlapping them to fit, and then return the dish to the oven. Cook until the filling is bubbling and the topping is deep golden brown and set, 20 to 30 minutes. Let the pandowdy cool for 10 minutes before serving.

Coconut is a trendy ingredient these days, and it seems that every day another expert is expounding the virtues of this tropical fruit. That's good news as far as I'm concerned—I just love the taste. My family from Sri Lanka, the island where coconut is in practically every dish, made me the coconut-lover I am today.

This beauty has everything you'd want in a carrot cake: a tender crumb, warm spices, and plenty of cream cheese frosting with the special addition of coconut. Coconut oil and a bit of coconut flour add a subtle tropical flavor to the downy cake without being overpowering.

SERVES 8 TO 12

BATTER

½ cup melted coconut oil, plus more for the pans (see Tip)

2½ cups (225 g) almond flour

½ cup (50 g) coconut flour

¼ cup cornstarch

2¼ teaspoons baking powder

½ teaspoon baking soda

2 teaspoons ground cinnamon

½ teaspoon freshly grated nutmeg

¼ teaspoon ground allspice

1 teaspoon kosher salt

1 cup packed dark brown sugar

½ cup whole milk, at room temperature

¼ cup granulated sugar

6 large eggs, at room temperature, separated

3 large carrots, peeled and grated (2½ cups)

⅔ cup golden raisins

⅔ cup chopped pecans

2 teaspoons pure vanilla extract

carrot cake with coconut cream cheese frosting

1 Prepare the batter: Preheat the oven to 350°F. Oil two 9-inch cake pans with coconut oil and line them with parchment rounds. In a large bowl, whisk together the almond flour, coconut flour, cornstarch, baking powder, baking soda, cinnamon, nutmeg, allspice, and salt.

2 In a large bowl, whisk together the brown sugar, milk, granulated sugar, egg yolks, and coconut oil. Stir in the carrots, raisins, pecans, and vanilla. Fold the carrot mixture into the almond flour mixture.

3 In another large bowl, beat the egg whites to stiff but not dry peaks. Stir about one third of the egg whites into the mixture to loosen it. Then gently fold in the remaining egg whites.

4 Transfer the batter to the prepared cake pans and bake until the cakes are golden brown and the center springs back when pressed very gently, 28 to 32 minutes. (A toothpick may come out clean before the cake is properly baked.)

(RECIPE CONTINUES)

FROSTING

2 8-ounce packages cream cheese,
at room temperature

½ cup coconut oil,
at room temperature (see Tip)

¾ cup confectioners' sugar

2 teaspoons pure vanilla extract

½ teaspoon kosher salt

5 Let the cakes cool in the pans on wire racks for 5 minutes. Then run a knife around the edge of both cakes and turn them out onto the racks to cool completely.

6 **Make the frosting:** In a large bowl, with an electric mixer, beat the cream cheese and coconut oil together until fluffy, about 3 minutes. Add the confectioners' sugar, vanilla, and salt, and beat for 2 minutes to combine.

7 **Assemble the cake:** Transfer one cooled cake to a serving plate. Spread about ¾ cup of the frosting over the top of the cake. Top with another cooled cake layer. Spread the remaining frosting all over the cake. Store any leftover cake in an airtight container at room temperature for up to 3 days.

---

tip It's easiest to measure coconut oil in its liquid state. If it isn't already liquid, run the closed jar under hot water or simply remove the lid and give it a few very short bursts in the microwave. Just let the oil cool to room temperature before proceeding with the recipe.

Woo some friends today by making them a cheesecake. A simple-to-prepare dessert, cheesecake is otherworldly in its powers—it can make people's eyes close at first bite. They forget about calories. They lose interest in conversation. They just want to have a long moment with each fluffy, creamy, ethereal taste.

chocolate and orange cheesecake

SERVES 10

CRUST

2½ cups gluten-free "graham" cracker crumbs (see page 164)

2 tablespoons unsalted butter, melted

1 tablespoon granulated sugar

½ teaspoon kosher salt

FILLING

3 8-ounce packages cream cheese, at room temperature

¾ cup granulated sugar

2 teaspoons finely grated orange zest (from 1 orange)

Pinch of kosher salt

1 cup sour cream, at room temperature

1 tablespoon cornstarch

3 large eggs, lightly beaten, at room temperature

2 ounces chopped bittersweet chocolate

Confectioners' sugar, chocolate shavings, or orange slices, for garnish (optional)

tip To easily remove the cheesecake from the springform pan, give the sides and the underside of the cake a quick blast with a blow-dryer. The heat will soften the butter in the crust just enough to release it from the pan.

1 Prepare the crust: Preheat the oven to 350°F. In a bowl, toss together the cracker crumbs, butter, sugar, and salt. Press the crumbs onto the bottom and about 1 inch up the sides of a 9-inch springform pan. Use a small flat-bottomed measuring cup to neatly press the crumbs onto the bottom and sides of the pan.

2 Bake the crust until it is fragrant and set, 8 to 12 minutes. Transfer the crust to a rack to cool completely. Reduce the oven temperature to 300°F.

3 Make the filling: Beat the cream cheese, sugar, orange zest, and salt with an electric mixer on medium speed until creamy and fluffy, about 3 minutes. Add the sour cream and the cornstarch, and beat until smooth.

4 Beat in the eggs until just combined, being careful not to overmix the batter. Fold in the chocolate. Transfer the batter to the cooled crust and smooth the top.

5 Bake until the edges of the cheesecake are set and very slightly puffed but the center still jiggles a bit when nudged gently, 40 to 50 minutes. Transfer the pan to a rack and let the cheesecake cool to room temperature; then cover and refrigerate until completely cooled, at least 8 hours and up to 2 days. Remove the pan edges and transfer the cheesecake to a platter to serve. Top with confectioners' sugar, chocolate shavings, or orange slices, if you like.

What's better than a dense, fudgy chocolate brownie? One that's topped with a chewy toasted coconut macaroon. This recipe gives you the best of two worlds in one sweet treat—great for the indecisive dessert-lover in your life. To get the richest flavors, look for coarsely shredded unsweetened coconut and dark bittersweet chocolate. I like something with around 70% cacao.

macaroon brownies

BATTER

8 tablespoons (1 stick) unsalted butter, cut into pieces, plus more for the pan

¾ cup (70 g) almond flour

2 tablespoons unsweetened Dutch-process cocoa powder

2 tablespoons arrowroot starch

1 teaspoon kosher salt

8 ounces bittersweet chocolate, chopped

⅔ cup sugar

2 teaspoons pure vanilla extract

3 large eggs

1 cup chopped pecans (optional)

TOPPING

2 cups coarsely shredded unsweetened coconut

⅓ cup sugar

1 large egg

½ teaspoon pure vanilla extract

¼ teaspoon kosher salt

1 **Start the batter:** Preheat the oven to 350°F. Butter a 9-inch square baking pan and line it with parchment, leaving a 2-inch overhang on two sides. Butter the paper. In a medium bowl, whisk together the almond flour, cocoa powder, arrowroot starch, and salt.

2 In a double boiler or large heatproof bowl set over a pot of barely simmering water, melt the chocolate and the butter together. Remove the bowl from the heat and stir until smooth. Whisk in the sugar and the vanilla. Then whisk in the eggs, one at a time. Stir in the almond flour mixture, and then the nuts if using. Transfer the batter to the prepared pan and bake until the top is set but the center is still moist, about 15 minutes.

3 **Meanwhile, prepare the topping:** In a medium bowl, stir together the coconut, sugar, egg, vanilla, and salt.

4 Remove the brownie from the oven and carefully dollop the coconut mixture over the top. Use an offset spatula to spread out the coconut mixture evenly. Return the pan to the oven and bake until the coconut is golden brown and set and a toothpick inserted into the center of the cake comes out with very moist crumbs attached, 18 to 20 minutes.

5 Set the pan on a rack to cool completely. Then cut around the edges of the pan and lift the brownie out, using the parchment as a handle. Remove the parchment and cut the brownie into pieces. Store the brownies in an airtight container for up to 2 days at room temperature or up to 1 month in the freezer.

These soft, chewy bars marry the beloved brown sugar flavor of a chocolate chip cookie with the silky richness of a tender sheet cake. Since it straddles the line between cookie and cake, eat it with your hands or on a plate with a fork—just be sure to eat it with friends.

blondie bars

MAKES 24 BARS

12 tablespoons (1½ sticks) unsalted butter, melted and cooled slightly, plus more for the pan

1½ cups (135 g) almond flour

⅓ cup (45 g) brown rice flour

⅓ cup (30 g) coconut flour

¼ cup tapioca starch

1 teaspoon baking soda

1 teaspoon kosher salt

1 cup packed dark brown sugar

½ cup granulated sugar

3 large eggs, at room temperature

1 tablespoon pure vanilla extract

1 cup pecans or walnuts, toasted and coarsely chopped

4 ounces bittersweet chocolate, chopped

1 Preheat the oven to 350°F. Butter a 9 × 13-inch baking pan and line it with parchment, leaving a 2-inch overhang on two sides. Butter the paper.

2 In a large bowl, whisk together the almond flour, brown rice flour, coconut flour, tapioca starch, baking soda, and salt. In a medium bowl, whisk together the butter, brown sugar, and granulated sugar until smooth and shiny. Add the eggs, one at a time, whisking after each addition. Then whisk in the vanilla.

3 Add the butter mixture to the almond flour mixture and stir to combine. Fold in the nuts and the chocolate. Transfer the batter to the prepared pan and smooth the top. Bake until a toothpick comes out clean, 24 to 26 minutes.

4 Set the pan to a rack to cool completely. Then, cut around the edges of the pan and lift the blondie out, using the parchment as a handle. Transfer the blondie to a cutting board, remove the parchment, and cut the blondie into bars. Store the blondies in an airtight container for up to 2 days at room temperature or up to 1 month in the freezer.

This pudding is dedicated to my little friend Benji. He's a chocolate-lover and happens to be my number one pudding taste-tester. You'll be glad to know that this dark chocolate tapioca got two messy thumbs-up and a lick of the bowl for good measure.

Plenty of cocoa powder and melted bittersweet chocolate make this a pudding that will appeal to any age, from one year to one century. Espresso powder enhances the deep chocolate flavor, but parents, feel free to leave it out if caffeine is a concern for your kids.

dark chocolate tapioca pudding

SERVES 4 TO 6 (MAKES 4 CUPS)

¼ cup small pearl tapioca

⅓ cup sugar

¼ cup unsweetened Dutch-process cocoa powder

2 teaspoons instant espresso powder (optional)

1 teaspoon kosher salt

2 large egg yolks

3 cups whole milk, plus more for serving

4 ounces bittersweet chocolate, melted

1 tablespoon pure vanilla extract

1 In a medium pot, combine the tapioca and 1 cup of water. Let stand for 30 minutes. Meanwhile, in a medium bowl, whisk together the sugar, cocoa powder, espresso powder if using, and salt. Set aside. Lightly beat the egg yolks in a heatproof bowl, and set it aside.

2 Drain the tapioca and return it to the pot. Add the milk and bring the mixture to a simmer. Cook, stirring occasionally to make sure the tapioca pearls aren't sticking to the bottom of the pot, until the pearls have swollen, 3 to 5 minutes. Add the sugar mixture and cook, stirring constantly, until it has dissolved, 1 to 2 minutes more.

3 While whisking, ladle about ½ cup of the hot milk mixture into the egg yolks. Repeat this process a few times to heat the yolks, and then return the mixture to the pot and stir to combine. Cook the mixture just until the egg yolks have fully cooked and the mixture has thickened, 30 seconds to 1 minute. Remove the pot from the heat and stir in the melted chocolate and the vanilla.

4 Serve the pudding warm or cold. To serve it cold, transfer it to a bowl and let it cool slightly. Then cover it with plastic wrap, making sure the plastic touches the surface of the pudding, and chill until cold. Stir a few tablespoons of milk into the cold pudding if you'd like a looser consistency.

These bars make the sugar-bomb treats we used to bake as children seem like kids' stuff. Instead of marshmallows, I like to use honey and a bit of brown sugar for a more complex, controlled sweetness.

crispy chocolate–peanut butter bars

MAKES 24 BARS

5 cups gluten-free crispy brown rice cereal

½ cup mild honey

¼ cup packed light brown sugar

¾ cup smooth, unsweetened natural peanut butter

½ teaspoon kosher salt

6 ounces semisweet chocolate, melted

1 Pour the cereal into a large heatproof bowl and set it aside. Line an 8-inch square baking pan with parchment, leaving a 2-inch overhang on two sides. In a small saucepan with a candy thermometer attached, heat the honey and brown sugar over medium heat until the temperature reaches 248°F, 3 to 4 minutes. If the sugar mixture is too low in the pan, the temperature won't register properly on the thermometer. To fix this, hold the pan at an angle while it cooks so the thermometer stays in the sugar mixture.

2 Immediately stir in the peanut butter and salt until smooth. Add the peanut butter mixture to the cereal and stir to coat it evenly. Transfer the mixture to the prepared pan and press it down evenly. Top with the melted chocolate and smooth the top. Let stand until the chocolate is set.

3 Using the parchment, pull the bar out of the pan and transfer it to a cutting board. Cut it into 24 pieces. Store in an airtight container for up to 1 week.

If you like Nutella, you'll love these simple cookies. With so few ingredients, the pure, sweet flavor of the hazelnuts really shines. I like using chocolate filling, but feel free to switch it with delicious jam. Add it at the beginning of step 1, just before baking.

hazelnut thumbprint cookies

MAKES ABOUT 2½ DOZEN COOKIES

9 tablespoons (1 stick plus 1 tablespoon) unsalted butter, at room temperature

½ cup confectioners' sugar

2 large egg yolks

2 cups (180 g) hazelnut flour

½ teaspoon ground cinnamon

½ teaspoon kosher salt

4 ounces semisweet chocolate, chopped

⅓ cup heavy cream

1 Preheat the oven to 350°F. In a large bowl, mix 8 tablespoons (1 stick) of the butter with the confectioners' sugar until combined. Stir in the egg yolks. Add the hazelnut flour, cinnamon, and salt and stir to combine.

2 Scoop level tablespoons of the dough onto two parchment-lined baking sheets, spacing them about 1 inch apart. Roll the dough into balls and then make an indentation in the center of each ball with a small measuring spoon. Freeze the cookies on the sheets for 10 minutes.

3 Bake the cookies until they are just set but still soft, about 8 minutes. Carefully remove the baking sheets from the oven and reinforce the wells with the measuring spoon. Rotate the sheets, return them to the oven, and continue to bake until the cookies are golden around the edges, 8 to 10 minutes. Let the cookies cool on the baking sheets on a wire rack for 5 minutes. Then use a spatula to transfer the cookies to the rack to cool completely.

4 Set the chocolate and the remaining tablespoon of butter in a small heatproof bowl. Heat the cream to a boil and then immediately pour it over the chocolate. Let the mixture stand for 2 minutes; then whisk until smooth. Transfer the mixture to a small resealable plastic bag, and let it cool for a few minutes until it firms up slightly.

5 Cut off one small corner of the plastic bag and gently squeeze some of the filling into the well of each cookie. Let the cookies stand until the filling is set. Store in an airtight container at room temperature for 1 week or in the freezer for up to 1 month.

Creating a good gluten-free loaf of bread was a challenge, to say the least. After testing loaf after loaf, I was swimming in half-eaten bread. It's good stuff, but one person can eat only so much! I realized I needed to develop a recipe to use up some of the leftovers. Bread pudding was the delicious answer. You'd be surprised how much warm, custardy bread pudding one seemingly full person can put away!

bread and butter pudding

SERVES 8

4 tablespoons (½ stick) unsalted butter, at room temperature, plus more for greasing the baking dish

8 slices gluten-free bread (see page 35), cut 1 inch thick

1½ cups heavy cream

1½ cups whole milk

4 large eggs

2 large egg yolks

¾ cup packed light brown sugar

1 teaspoon pure vanilla extract

1 teaspoon ground cinnamon

½ teaspoon kosher salt

½ cup golden raisins

¼ cup dried sour cherries

Confectioners' sugar, for dusting (optional)

1 Butter a 2-quart baking dish. Preheat the oven to 350°F. Spread the butter on both sides of each bread slice and then cut the bread into 1-inch cubes. Spread the cubes on a rimmed baking sheet and bake until lightly toasted, 10 to 15 minutes, tossing them halfway through.

2 In a large bowl, whisk together the cream, milk, whole eggs, egg yolks, brown sugar, vanilla, cinnamon, and salt. Transfer the toasted bread cubes to the prepared baking dish and pour the cream mixture over them. Sprinkle the raisins and cherries on top, and stir gently to disperse them. Cover with plastic wrap and store in the refrigerator for about 1 hour.

3 Preheat the oven to 350°F. Bring a kettle of water to a boil. Remove the plastic and set the baking dish in a large roasting pan. Fill the roasting pan with enough boiling water to reach about halfway up the sides of the baking dish. Carefully place the pan in the oven and bake until the custard is set (even in the very center) and the pudding has puffed slightly, 45 to 50 minutes.

4 Remove the pan from the oven, let it cool slightly, and then remove the baking dish from the water. Serve the pudding warm, dusted with confectioners' sugar if desired.

cinnamon ice cream, page 188

Crispy oat cookies dotted with chunks of melted chocolate and sandwiched around extra-creamy cinnamon ice cream—this is the stuff of summer dreams. If you're in a hurry, crumble the cookies over bowls of ice cream and call it a day. Or, simply serve the cookies on their own. No one will complain.

oatmeal–chocolate chunk ice cream sandwiches

MAKES ABOUT 1½ DOZEN SANDWICHES

¼ cup oat flour

¼ cup almond flour

½ teaspoon baking powder

¼ teaspoon baking soda

¼ teaspoon ground cinnamon

½ teaspoon kosher salt

½ cup packed dark brown sugar

¼ cup granulated sugar

8 tablespoons (1 stick) unsalted butter, at room temperature

1 large egg, at room temperature

½ teaspoon pure vanilla extract

1½ cups old-fashioned rolled oats

2 ounces chopped bittersweet chocolate

½ cup chopped walnuts or raisins (optional)

1 batch Cinnamon Ice Cream (page 188), softened slightly

1 In a small bowl, combine the oat flour, almond flour, baking powder, baking soda, cinnamon, and salt. In a large bowl, using a wooden spoon, combine the brown sugar, granulated sugar, and butter. Stir in the egg and the vanilla.

2 Add the flour mixture to the butter mixture and stir to combine. Then add the oats, chocolate, and nuts or raisins if using. Scoop 1-tablespoon mounds of the dough onto a parchment-lined baking sheet. Freeze them on the baking sheet for 20 minutes and then roll the scoops into neat balls. Preheat the oven to 375°F.

3 Set the balls 2 inches apart on two parchment-lined baking sheets. Flatten each ball slightly with the palm of your hand. Bake until the cookies are set and the edges are golden brown, 8 to 10 minutes, rotating the sheets halfway through. Let the cookies cool for 5 minutes, and then transfer them to a rack to cool completely.

4 To assemble the sandwiches, top the flat side of half of the cookies with about 3 tablespoons of ice cream each. Top with another cookie, flat side down. Set the sandwiches on a cookie sheet and transfer it to the freezer for up to 6 hours. Once they are solid, you can serve them or wrap them up tightly in plastic wrap and keep them in the freezer until ready to eat. They'll keep this way for up to 1 week.

This ice cream is magic. Sweet cream ice cream with just the right amount of ground cinnamon—the final product is so much more than the sum of its parts. The heat of the cinnamon blooms in the custard base and becomes mellow and smooth. It's a perfect filling for the ice cream sandwiches (page 187) or topping for the Upside-Down Plum Cake (page 193) . . . or simply eat it out of the container with a spoon and a smile.

cinnamon ice cream

MAKES ABOUT 6 CUPS

6 large egg yolks

½ cup sugar

Pinch of kosher salt

2 cups heavy cream

1½ cups whole milk

1 teaspoon ground cinnamon

1 teaspoon pure vanilla extract

1 In a medium heatproof bowl, whisk together the egg yolks, sugar, and salt. In a medium saucepan, bring the cream, ½ cup of the milk, and the cinnamon to a simmer over medium heat. Meanwhile, pour the remaining 1 cup milk and the vanilla into a large bowl. Set a fine-mesh sieve over the bowl.

2 While whisking, slowly add the warm cream mixture to the yolk mixture. Return the mixture to the pot and cook over medium-low heat, stirring constantly, until it is just thick enough to coat the back of a spoon, 6 to 8 minutes.

3 Strain the mixture through the sieve into the large bowl of milk, and discard any solids. Stir the mixture thoroughly. Chill the ice cream base until it is completely cold. (Or set it over a bowl of ice water if you're in a hurry.)

4 Freeze the chilled base in an ice cream maker according to the manufacturer's instructions. Spoon the ice cream into a freezer-proof container and freeze until firm, at least 8 hours.

5 Let the ice cream sit at room temperature for about 10 minutes before serving. Store it in an airtight container, with a layer of plastic wrap pressed directly onto the surface of the ice cream, in the freezer for up to 2 weeks.

This is the perfect dessert for when you want something warm and sweet but haven't planned ahead. It takes only a few minutes to whip up but looks mighty impressive and tastes wonderfully decadent, especially with a scoop of unsweetened freshly whipped cream or Cinnamon Ice Cream (page 188).

warm chocolate mousse cakes

SERVES 4

4 ounces bittersweet chocolate, chopped

2 tablespoons unsalted butter

2 large eggs, separated

1 teaspoon pure vanilla extract

2 tablespoons arrowroot starch

½ teaspoon kosher salt

3 tablespoons sugar

Unsweetened whipped cream, for serving

1 Preheat the oven to 325°F. In a double boiler or medium heatproof bowl set over a pot of barely simmering water, or in short bursts in the microwave, melt the chocolate and butter together. Stir to combine, and then set aside to cool for a minute or two. Then stir in the egg yolks, vanilla, arrowroot starch, and salt.

2 In a large clean bowl, with an electric mixer, beat the egg whites to soft peaks. Gradually add the sugar and beat until stiff, shiny peaks form, about 2 minutes. Stir a scoop of the egg whites into the chocolate mixture to loosen it; then carefully fold the remaining egg whites into the chocolate mixture.

3 Divide the batter among four 4-ounce ramekins and smooth the tops. Set the ramekins on a baking sheet, and bake until the cakes are puffed and the tops look dry, 24 to 28 minutes. Serve warm, topped with whipped cream.

These are infinitely better than the store-bought version. Homemade candy is always tastier because you can use the good-quality ingredients, like artisanal chocolate and real vanilla beans, that big candy manufacturers wouldn't dream of spending money on. To make these guys extra-special, I've toasted the coconut. I love almonds, but if you don't, feel free to omit the nuts.

toasty coconut almond candies

MAKES ABOUT 2 DOZEN CANDIES

3½ cups unsweetened shredded coconut

¼ cup coconut oil, melted (see Tip, page 175)

1 vanilla bean, split, seeds scraped out and reserved

5 tablespoons Lyle's Golden Syrup (see Tip)

¼ teaspoon coarse salt

¼ to ½ cup roasted salted almonds

12 ounces bittersweet chocolate

tip I love Lyle's Golden Syrup, the thick, richly flavored syrup made from sugar cane. Nowadays, this British staple is easy to find in a well-stocked supermarket. While honey can usually be substituted for Lyle's, I don't suggest using honey in this recipe as the flavor is too strong.

1 In a large skillet, toast the coconut over medium heat, stirring constantly, until it is golden brown, 8 to 10 minutes. Transfer the toasted coconut to the bowl of a food processor.

2 Add the coconut oil and the vanilla bean seeds to the same skillet and warm over low heat, 1 to 2 minutes. Scrape the coconut oil mixture into the bowl of the food processor. Add the Lyle's Golden Syrup and the salt. Process until the mixture is well combined and the coconut is finely chopped. Transfer the mixture to a bowl and let it stand until completely cool. (The mixture will hold together once the coconut oil cools down.)

3 Line a baking sheet or a plate (depending on how much room you have in your freezer) with parchment. Using your hands, firmly squeeze the mixture into about twenty-four 1½ × 1-inch ovals and set them on the prepared sheet. Press one or two almonds into each oval, taking care to reshape it if necessary. Transfer the sheet to the freezer and freeze until the candies are very firm, at least 30 minutes.

(RECIPE CONTINUES)

4 While the candies are chilling, chop the chocolate and melt it in a double boiler or small heatproof bowl set over a pot of barely simmering water. Using two forks, drop a candy into the melted chocolate and toss to coat it. Use a fork to lift the candy out of the chocolate, tap it against the edge of the bowl to allow the excess chocolate to drip off, and then set the candy on the same parchment-lined baking sheet. Repeat with the remaining candies.

5 Chill the candies for 30 minutes, until they are set, and then transfer them to an airtight container and store them in the fridge for up to a week or in the freezer for up to a month.

This rustic beauty is extremely adaptable. I love it with the caramelized red plums, but if you happen to have some peaches on hand, or some in-season apricots, try it with them. In the fall, bake it up hot and bubbly with pears or apples. I'm in love with almond extract, but if you're more of a vanilla fan, feel free to make the switch. Whatever you wish, this custardy, fruity cake always delivers.

upside-down plum cake

SERVES 10

FRUIT LAYER

8 firm red plums, pitted and cut into quarters (see Tip, page 195)

⅓ cup plus 2 tablespoons sugar

3 tablespoons unsalted butter

Pinch of kosher salt

BATTER

1½ cups (135 g) almond flour

2 tablespoons arrowroot starch

1½ teaspoons baking powder

½ teaspoon kosher salt

4 tablespoons (½ stick) unsalted butter, at room temperature

½ cup sugar

4 large eggs, separated

1 teaspoon pure almond extract

1 Make the fruit layer: In a large fine-mesh strainer set over a bowl, toss the plums with the 2 tablespoons of sugar. Set aside for at least 30 minutes to drain off some of the excess juice. (Add the accumulated juice to a glass of sparkling water.)

2 In a 10-inch oven-safe skillet, melt the butter over medium heat. Add the remaining ⅓ cup sugar and the salt and cook, swirling the skillet, until the sugar has melted and turned into a golden brown caramel, about 3 minutes. (Don't worry if the caramel separates. It will come together in the next step.) Remove the skillet from the heat, carefully add the plums, and toss to coat. Cook just until the caramel has smoothed out, about 30 seconds. Remove the skillet from the heat and set it aside.

3 Prepare the batter: Preheat the oven to 350°F, with a piece of foil placed on the bottom rack to catch any drips. In a medium bowl, whisk together the almond flour, arrowroot starch, baking powder, and salt. Using an electric mixer in another medium bowl, beat the butter and sugar until fluffy and well combined, about 3 minutes. Add the egg yolks and the almond extract, and beat to combine. Add the almond flour mixture to the butter mixture and beat to combine. The batter will be stiff.

(RECIPE CONTINUES)

4 In a clean bowl, with clean beaters, beat the egg whites to stiff but not dry peaks, about 2 minutes. Stir about a third of the egg whites into the almond flour mixture to loosen it, and then fold in the remaining whites. Transfer the batter to the skillet, and smooth the top.

5 Bake until the cake is golden brown and a toothpick inserted into the center comes out with moist crumbs attached, 35 to 40 minutes. Let the cake cool in the skillet on a wire rack for 10 minutes. Then carefully flip the cake over onto a serving plate. Serve warm or at room temperature.

---

tip In the summer, when the plums are super-juicy, I like to set them aside with some sugar to let the excess juice drain off. Omit this step if your plums aren't so wet.

My friend Liz first introduced me to pitted Medjool dates stuffed with mascarpone cheese. She brought a tray out at the end of a dinner party. We nibbled while we finished our wine and I couldn't stop gushing. It's genius. Creamy, buttery cheese tucked into chewy, sweet dates is one of the most satisfying desserts around. I now make these for myself often.

For this recipe, I took the idea a few steps further. Warm dates oozing with cheese and topped with toasty nuts, flaky salt, and a few sparkling, tart pomegranate arils make a memorable dessert with barely any effort.

stuffed dates with pomegranate and honey

SERVES 4 TO 6

12 plump dried Medjool dates, pitted but not halved (see Tip)

2 tablespoons extra virgin olive oil

½ cup mascarpone cheese, at room temperature

1 to 2 teaspoons honey

3 to 4 tablespoons pomegranate arils

3 to 4 tablespoons chopped toasted walnuts

Flaky sea salt, for sprinkling

1 Preheat the oven to 350°F. Set the dates in a small baking dish and drizzle the olive oil over them. Bake until the dates are soft and warm throughout, 12 to 15 minutes.

2 Let the dates cool slightly. Then fill each date with a bit of mascarpone. Top the dates with the honey, pomegranate arils, walnuts, and a bit of flaky salt. Serve hot.

***

tip To remove the pit from a date, make a small slit in the top of the fruit with a paring knife. Then use the tip of the knife to lift the pit up out of the hole and pull it out completely with your fingers.

This is a luscious and simple tart, perfect for when raspberries are plentiful and the heat of the oven is bearable for only a short time. I use ground almonds to make the crust, but feel free to substitute a scant 2 cups (175 g) of almond flour if you have it on hand.

raspberry cream tart with pistachios

SERVES 8 TO 10

CRUST

2 tablespoons unsalted butter, melted, plus more for the tart pan

1¼ cups raw almonds

½ cup shelled raw pistachios

⅓ cup sugar

½ teaspoon kosher salt

1 large egg yolk

FILLING

4 large egg yolks

¼ cup sugar

2 tablespoons cornstarch

Pinch of kosher salt

1¼ cups whole milk

¾ cup heavy cream

1 vanilla bean, split, seeds scraped out and reserved

2 tablespoons unsalted butter

1 Prepare the crust: Preheat the oven to 350°F. Butter a 9-inch fluted tart pan with a removable bottom or a standard 9-inch pie plate. Combine the almonds, pistachios, sugar, and salt in the bowl of a food processor and pulse until the nuts are very finely ground. Add the melted butter and the egg yolk, and pulse until the nut mixture is evenly moistened.

2 Tip the nut mixture out into the prepared tart pan and press it evenly over the bottom and sides. Set the pan on a baking sheet and bake until the crust is light brown and set, about 15 minutes. Transfer the pan to a rack to cool completely.

3 Make the filling: Place a fine-mesh sieve over a large heatproof bowl, and set it aside. In another heatproof bowl, whisk together the egg yolks, sugar, cornstarch, and salt. In a medium saucepan, bring the milk, cream, and vanilla bean and seeds to a simmer over medium-low heat. Carefully ladle about ¼ cup of the hot milk mixture into the yolk mixture, and whisk to combine. Repeat this process a few times until most of the milk mixture has been incorporated. Return the yolk mixture to the saucepan.

(RECIPE CONTINUES)

TOPPING

1½ cups fresh raspberries

1 tablespoon sugar

½ cup chopped shelled raw
pistachios

4 Heat the custard over medium heat, stirring constantly, until the mixture begins to thicken, 3 to 4 minutes. Bring it to a very low boil and cook for another minute, stirring constantly. Remove the pan from the heat and strain the custard through the sieve into the clean bowl.

5 Add the butter to the hot custard, let it melt, and then stir it in. Pour the custard into the prepared crust. Chill the tart until the custard has set, 1 to 2 hours.

6 Finish the tart: Shortly before serving, toss the raspberries with the sugar in a small bowl, and let them stand for 10 minutes. Top the tart with the raspberries and any accumulated juices, and sprinkle with the pistachios.

I like to serve this dish for dessert, but really, with oats, fruit, and maple syrup, you could make a strong argument for having it at breakfast: try the crisp heaped over a bowl of plain yogurt. The combination of sweet, tart, and ginger is perfect any time of the day.

pear and ginger crisp

SERVES 8

5 ripe Bartlett or Anjou pears (about 2½ pounds), peeled, cored, and cut into ½-inch-thick wedges

1 tablespoon minced peeled fresh ginger

¼ cup maple syrup (see Tip)

1 tablespoon cornstarch

1 cup old-fashioned rolled oats

¼ cup packed light or dark brown sugar

¾ cup chopped pecans

½ teaspoon kosher salt

4 tablespoons (½ stick) unsalted butter, at room temperature

1 Preheat the oven to 350°F. In an 8-inch square baking dish, combine the pears, ginger, maple syrup, and cornstarch, and toss to combine.

2 In a medium bowl, combine the oats, brown sugar, pecans, and salt. Knead in the butter with your fingers just until the oat mixture is evenly moistened. Sprinkle the oat mixture over the pears.

3 Bake until the topping is golden brown, the pears are tender, and the juices are bubbling, 35 to 45 minutes. Serve warm.

---

tip If your pears are very sweet, feel free to dial back the maple syrup by a tablespoon or so.

acknowledgments

I owe the most sincere thanks to many extraordinary people who had a hand (and a spoon) in creating this book.

First and foremost, to Laurie Buckle. She believed in me way back when, hired me for a job I probably wasn't quite qualified for, and then gave me many opportunities to shine. Thank you for trusting me with this project. I hope you're proud of the results.

Thank you to my beloved team of recipe testers: Jenny Abramson, Erin Chapman, B Chatfield, Eddy Dibner, Paulie Dibner, Jessica Fox, Deborah Keefe, Amy Leo, Cathy Lo, Sarah Rosenthal, Jason Schreiber, Abby Simchak, Nicki Sizemore, Martha Tinkler, and Merritt Watts made each one of these recipes better than it was before. I'm so grateful for your help.

To Stephen Kent Johnson for these beautiful images, Sarah Smart and Beatrice Chastka for their prop wizardry, and Jessie Damuck and Katie Stilo for cooking like a dream. Who knew a photo shoot could be so much fun? Let's always dance while we work.

I often wonder how I tricked Janis Donnaud into signing me. She's the best agent a girl could ask for.

So many thanks to Angelin Borsics, La Tricia Watford, Cathy Hennessy, Kim Tyner, Natasha Martin, Lauren Velasquez, and the entire Clarkson Potter team. I think we've done something good.

To Mom and Dad for being lovable.

And to all the genius gluten-free chefs, recipe developers, and eaters who came before me. You paved the way and made millet flour easy to find. Thank you.

index

Note: Page references in *italics* indicate photographs.